D0810156

RISK

Rev o*lu"tion , n.: a drastic and far-reaching change in ways of thinking and behaving

REVOLUTION

THE THREATS FACING AMERICA & TECHNOLOGY'S PROMISE FOR A SAFER TOMORROW

DEREK V. SMITH

LONGSTREET PRESS
Atlanta, Georgia

LONGSTREET
PRESS

Published by
LONGSTREET PRESS, INC.
2974 Hardman Court
Atlanta, Georgia 30305
www.longstreetpress.net

Copyright © 2004 ChoicePoint Asset Company

1st printing, 2004

ISBN: 1-56352-734-0

All rights reserved. No part of this book may be reproduced in any form
or by any means without the prior written permission of the Publisher,
excepting brief quotes used in connection with reviews, written
specifically for inclusion in a magazine or newspaper.

Printed in the United States of America

Book design by Burtch Hunter Design LLC

"Nine-tenths of wisdom consists of being wise in time."

THEODORE ROOSEVELT

RISK

Rev o*lu"tion , n.: a drastic and far-reaching change in ways of thinking and behaving

REVOLUTION

TABLE OF CONTENTS

FOREWORD

Suppose you and your spouse decide to hire someone to look after your new baby. Wouldn't you want to know if the well-spoken woman with the bright smile who answers your ad has convictions in two states for child abuse?

In the world in which Derek Smith grew up, his parents would probably know that – because it's likely they'd be hiring someone from the neighborhood everyone knew. But, as Smith explains in this important book, the world most of us live in today isn't like that. Most of us don't know our neighbors, and we aren't tied, as the generation before us was, to the kinds of local institutions – be it the candy store or the local church – that were the staples of our parents' lives. People move around more, seeking jobs and opportunity in an increasingly complex, fast-moving economy. Even small towns are not so small.

It's not that life is necessarily worse. It's just different. But what's also different is the opportunity provided by technology to fill the information gaps created, in this case, by the absence of a local grapevine that would give you the scoop on your would-be nanny.

Derek Smith, the CEO of ChoicePoint, has built a great business filling those information gaps. Now, he has written a book that lays out the case for how we can continue to take advantage of these kinds of data and information technology breakthroughs to provide comfort and security in an increasingly uncertain world.

One of the products Smith's company produces allows you or me to spend a few dollars online and check to see if that nanny is a convicted child abuser. Others allow DNA science to free the innocent and convict the guilty, or allow the government and private companies to screen job applicants seeking positions of high responsibility and risk.

As Smith points out, what ChoicePoint has built, and the "data-analysis" empire it and its competitors represent, is highly controversial. Often the controversy is expressed as a battle between "privacy" and "security." But in the case of the nanny, this really isn't true. If the nanny had been convicted of crimes, she has no right to keep that private. Indeed, the Constitution requires that all court proceedings be public. And the rest of us have a right to know what goes on in court. What ChoicePoint has done in this case is nothing more and nothing less than allowing us all an easy way to go to every courthouse in the country, as would be our right, to search public records to see if the nanny is a convict.

That is not to say that the issues Smith covers in the pages that follow are always that simple. This is what makes his straightforward argument that we have to harness the promise of information so intriguing, and, I hope, is the beginning of a debate that our country needs to have. We might feel differently about a father of three searching for a job to feed his family who doesn't get hired because ten years ago he was convicted of drug possession and his would-be employer doesn't believe in redemption. Or we might feel differently about insurance companies or banks setting our insurance or credit rates based on their ability, via ChoicePoint, to delve years back into our credit histories—to which they would reply that such information allows them to give lower rates to people with better risk or credit histories, while arming them with the information to ward off those who have a history of false insurance claims or credit defaults. And we almost certainly would feel uncomfortable or worse about the prospect of for-profit companies having warehouses full of information for sale to anyone and everyone on what we buy, where we've traveled, where we've lived, and everything else about us. (ChoicePoint doesn't sell information that way, but the available technology certainly makes it possible.)

The first time I met Derek Smith, and we talked about these issues he stopped me cold with one statement: "There is a big difference," he said, "between privacy and anonymity. Yes, we have a right to privacy. But in this society we can't have a right to anonymity."

I think he's right. And I think as you follow the case he builds you'll agree. In an age where nineteen people could be living quietly among us, most with falsified identification papers of one kind or another, only to kill 3,000 of us on September 11, we need to be able to know who people really are so that we can get a handle on the risk they pose when they engage in activities—like buying firearms, or boarding airplanes, or working in chemical factories or in schools—that could endanger the rest of us. And, yes, we should be able to use the analytics that Smith and his competitors now do to tell us if the man about to sit next to us on a 747 once shared a phone number with one of the September 11 hijackers, used the credit card of another to rent a car, and had the same address for two years of a third member of that terrorist group. Maybe we'd still let him fly, but wouldn't we want to search him more carefully than the ten-year old standing in line behind him?

But how do we do that without delving into everyone's life? Without making all kinds of false connections? And without giving Smith a free pass to sell anyone and everyone information about what we read, who we sleep with, what health problems we have?

The answer is not to try to put the data revolution genie back in the bottle, thereby giving up on the advantages it offers us in an increasingly dangerous, anonymous world. Rather, we have to listen to people like Smith as he paints his vision of how this revolution can help us, and then listen to the critics as well. We need a robust national discussion about these issues, a discussion that I think ought to end with sensible, strong regulation so that privacy can be preserved while anonymity is stripped away from those who need it to hurt us.

The issues are more complicated than some of Smith's critics like to picture them. In the early 1990's, I founded Court TV and during that time crusaded to allow cameras in the courts so that the Constitution's promise of public trials could be fulfilled by the technological advances of cable television (and of cameras that required no special lighting or wires and, therefore, presented little chance of disrupting a courtroom). The New York Civil Liberties Union opposed us, arguing that televised trials would embarrass defendants and perhaps even pressure judges who would otherwise hand out more lenient sentences. I responded that when the Founding Fathers mandated public trials they didn't care about embarrassing defendants or making judges publicly accountable—indeed, that embarrassment and accountability is part of what a criminal justice system, not to mention a free press, is all about. In an ironic illustration of how complicated and difficult the issue really was, the New York Civil Liberties Union's national parent, the American Civil Liberties Union, sided with Court TV and against its own New York affiliate, because the ACLU appreciated the constitutional rights and values that televised trials redeemed. These are not issues that lend themselves to knee-jerk ideological positions.

The analogy here, it seems to me, is that by using the technology that Derek Smith describes so vividly in the pages that follow, we may end up safeguarding some rights rather than endangering them. For we will know who the real risks are. For example, rather than not hiring a nanny because we think she "looks" kind of risky, if we have the kind of real information Derek Smith is talking about, we can make a better, less prejudiced choice. Or rather than search everyone's briefcase or pocketbook at an entrance to a stadium or an office building, we might, if we had a system by which people could volunteer for advance background screening, make it so that those volunteers would not be searched. The result would be fewer invasive searches, which, it could be argued, means less invasions of privacy.

Which brings me to the conflict of interest I have in urging this book on you as something to read, talk about, and debate: Derek and ChoicePoint are my partners in a new business I have launched, Verified Identity Pass, that does exactly that kind of voluntary background screening so that people can get expedited security clearance through various checkpoints.

To be sure, I don't agree with everything Derek has written, and I think he should have been tougher when it comes to talking about how the work he is doing could be abused if run by people who, unlike him, would abuse it. For my money, with the success of a business like ChoicePoint ought to come federal regulations that put people in prison who intentionally violate their promises of protecting privacy and not selling this information to anyone and everyone who wants it. And CEO's like Smith—or me—ought to be personally on the hook for those violations. (Read what follows, and you'll know that Smith doesn't shrink from that responsibility, either.)

I suspect we'll be hearing more from Derek Smith on these issues. I hope so, because in this compelling, important book he's gotten off to a great start in leading the national discussion we have to have.

Steven Brill
January 24, 2004

DEDICATION

To my wife, Lisa, daughter Hanley, and son, Tanner
for your love, patience and inspiration.

AUTHOR'S NOTE

January 2004

"What worries keep you awake at night?" That question, asked by reporters in an annual ritual, is one of the things they don't prepare you for in business school. It's a simple enough question, but for me, it comes with a complex answer. One that has, in part, lead me to this moment and the completion of nearly two years of work putting on paper the ideas and philosophies that I've spent the better part of my life forming.

What keeps me awake at night is the knowledge that so many of the tragedies—small and large—that we see every day could have been prevented or reduced if only the right well-meaning person had the right information at the precise moment they needed it to make a well-informed decision. From the airline ticket agent who allowed the September 11th terrorists onto airplanes to the minister who allowed a convicted sex offender to lead Sunday School and Scout groups—seemingly minor decisions made without the benefit of modern information tools can go terribly awry.

It's my privilege to lead the company that is now the leading provider of many of these information tools—ChoicePoint. It may be my role as Chairman and CEO, but more importantly, it's my personal mission to help make our world a safer place through the use of technology. I've studied and helped nurture this passion into reality since I was a computer science and business student in the 1970s.

ChoicePoint is not a household name, nor do we aspire to be. What we do seek is to help create a safer, more secure world through the responsible use of information. In other words, we want to ensure the information available today is put to good use and in a way that respects and protects personal privacy, not invades or diminishes it. The vast majority of our business is with private companies, but we also work with more than 7,000 local, state, and federal law enforcement and homeland security agencies, other government agencies, and nonprofits. Our data is either permission-based, in that you agreed to your information being used in a consumer transaction like an insurance or job application, or it comes from a public document or source that any citizen has a right to access.

With few exceptions, our customers are not individuals. We do sell certain products to consumers, but the products are geared toward helping them reduce risk in their everyday lives or reviewing information that exists about them or their property. We do not allow curious browsing or sell data about one consumer to another without a person's permission, or in the case of a public record, a legally permissible purpose.

Occasionally, I will use anecdotes and statistics from work ChoicePoint has performed, but I try to do it in a nonobvious way. I want my association with ChoicePoint as a benefactor of information dissemination throughout society to be clear and transparent.

Critics might suggest this book is a veiled guise to either promote ChoicePoint or our products and services. It is not. When a company statistic or example is used, it's done so only to avoid having an uncredited source. When you see the name Bode Technology Group, be aware that this is a division of ChoicePoint. Database Technologies (DBT) and CDB Infotek are also companies we acquired. VolunteerSelect™, AutoTrackXP® and C.L.U.E.® are ChoicePoint products.

There is no personal financial motivation for me in the sale of this book. All of the proceeds due me will be held in escrow for donation to charities that work to increase the safety and security of women, children, the elderly and other vulnerable people or groups.

My goal is to prompt a national discussion. Since long before September 11, 2001, our world was becoming a riskier place to live, work, and do business. This book is all about that trend and what we can do to help restore a bit of the peace of mind we once took for granted.

I believe the solution lies in no small part in the information tools, used responsibly, that are now or will soon be available. But to keep these tools from being disabled by well-intentioned but ill-informed efforts, society must begin to discuss how, when, and by whom information tools will be employed in the future.

On one side of the debate are those people who would try to put the technological genie back in the bottle. On the other side, people who believe technology and information tools should be used free of any societal or legal regulation. Both sides are wrong.

I hope the battleground staked out in this book is the middle ground. A call for a clear-headed discussion of the valuable outcomes of information used the right way, so we can create a framework that also prevents and punishes the misuse of data.

I had a great deal of help and support with this book, starting with the more than 4,000 associates at ChoicePoint who bring to life, every day, the vision of helping to create a safer, more secure world through the responsible use of information.

Our team is a FOCUSed one—that is to say, we're Fun Loving, believe in Open Communication, we're Committed to Excellence, Unselfish in the time and energy we devote to each other and our communities, and dedicated to Success. For helping me refine my thoughts and keeping me true to our vision, several colleagues deserve specific recognition, Tom Bode, Richard Collier, David Davis, Dr. John Hamre, Michael de Janes, David Lee, Dr. Kevin McElfresh, Don McGuffey, Dave Pugmire, Deslie Webb Quinby, Lauren Waits, and Jim Zimbardi.

Several friends and respected business leaders provided insight and, frankly, challenged me on the thoughts and philosophies outlined here. My thanks to Robert Belair, John Deaver, Rod Dowling, Jeff Jonas, Dr. Ricardo

Martinez, Michael Reene, Russ Richards, and Howard Safir.

I'm grateful to Steven Brill, not only for contributing a stirring foreword, but for his contributions to the overall discussion of how to make our nation a safer place in an increasingly risky world.

James Lee is ChoicePoint's marketing leader, the person whose passion, dedication, and persistence brings us to today. Without his encouragement and support, this book might still be on my Things To Do list, not the reality you hold in your hand.

Mike Kami, my friend and mentor, is one of the most honorable and intelligent men I have ever had the privilege of meeting. He is an invaluable influence on my personal development and a guiding force in my pursuit of "the greater good" for society.

I would be remiss if I didn't thank Leah Williamson, my assistant. She is unflappable and the consummate professional when dealing with the daily challenges of running the chairman's office and helping to keep this project moving. She sets the bar of excellence very high.

The very best operating executive in our industry is Doug Curling, my partner in leading ChoicePoint for more than a decade now. Our relationship is more than lines on an organizational chart (which we don't have at ChoicePoint); we are a team that is greater than the sum of the parts.

And, finally, my deepest gratitude is reserved for Vince Coppola. For nearly two years, Vince has helped me take the concepts I've discussed for years and refine them into words on a page. What started as a professional partnership has evolved into a valued friendship. Vince's talent as a writer and teacher is surpassed only by his dedication to the proposition that we can use information and technology wisely, but only through careful, considered decisions.

PROLOGUE

I grew up in a small town. In the 1960s, America was still a nation of small towns. Sayville, on Long Island's Great South Bay, my town, mirrored thousands of other communities across the country, its history and traditions, commerce and demographics as clearly reflected as the images of shoppers strolling past the windows of The Charlotte Shop. In Sayville, some families had roots extending all the way back to the Dutch and English settlers who'd arrived in the mid-eighteenth century; others were more recent arrivals, middle income families from the teeming ethnic enclaves of Brooklyn and the Bronx dreaming of fresh air, green space, and small town community.

In the 1960s, Sayville's children lived a Stephen Spielberg idyll, zooming down Main Street, past bayside Victorians on our bicycles, playing baseball, lolling away summers at the beach. The thwack of the screen door closing at our backs was as familiar as the ping of today's incoming e-mail. Certainly, there were troubled families and pockets of need, but overall, as I recall, it was a hopeful time. Tom Brokaw would not coin the phrase for another 35 years, but we were the children of the Greatest Generation, those men and women who had given so much of themselves in the factories and battlefields of World War II to make the world safe for democracy. Growing up in our community's secure embrace, we couldn't imagine an America not loved, admired, or envied anywhere in the world.

In Sayville, you knew your neighbors, shopkeepers, and the cop on the beat. The family doctor, the minister, and occasionally a teacher, hoping to head off a failing grade, made house calls, part of a sophisticated communications network—long before fiber optics—that linked the community in a hundred ways. Some understated: a shared cup of coffee at

Beer's café where the discussion might center around who owned the new Oldsmobile parked outside, or who stayed too late, too often, at the office. Others vital: keeping an eye on each other's kids, patronizing community businesses, volunteering to coach the Little League teams. In those days, strangers weren't considered threats; they were neighbors you hadn't met, potential customers, weekend visitors escaping Manhattan's heat for the shore. My friends attended the same school-Sayville High—as I did, played on and rooted for the same teams, rode the Fire Island ferries. In Sayville, you tuned to WABC-TV or Manhattan's WINS all-news radio to find out what was happening in the world, but you also stopped by the filling station where Bud Van Wyen dispensed gossip with a tank of gas.

Beneath the calm surface, tectonic plates were slowly beginning to shift. The South was not yet the Sunbelt. Silicon Valley was still raw farmland. On Long Island, the great suburban migration was underway. Of my parents' generation, few were willing to abandon rhythms and routines, uproot themselves from friends and family, without tremendous soul-searching.

My parents still live in the house I grew up in. Don Smith, my father, never left Sayville. He was born upstate in Elmira, and raised by his elder sister in nearby Bayport-Bluepoint. My mother's family has been in Sayville for generations. The Vanderborghs were baymen dredging oysters, and then clams out of the Great South Bay. June, my mother, taught school. Don was a professor at Adelphi University in Garden City and later, head of the graduate education program at Dowling College in nearby Oakdale. Together, proof that a meaningful life does not have to be lived on a grand scale.

Many of my early memories swirl around my parents' involvement with their students, their determination to have a positive impact on other lives. Don graduated from Dartmouth in the gray flannel 1950s, but remains a diehard Democrat who has never lost sight of the fact that the world is filled with those less fortunate than he. June, a moderate Republican, played the organ at the West Sayville Dutch Reformed Church. Still a dynamo, she spends her time doing volunteer work. I wasn't conscious of it growing up-my thoughts ran to football and athletic glory—but their quiet example instilled a desire in me to serve something larger than self-interest and to never define success simply in economic terms. They had weathered the Depression, liberated Europe, raised families, and pursued happiness in the long shadow of the Cold War. They didn't need to constantly "reinvent" themselves or pull up roots except to answer a military call or the siren song of the Fortune 500. In 2002 the New York Times described Sayville as "homey and pleasantly retro." In 1962, retro was reality.

Over the next 30 years, everything changed. Looking back, I recall a blur of issues, opportunities, personalities, movements and events accelerated by dizzying advances in communications and technology. Looking closer, I've come to understand the changes that swept our nation were nothing less than revolutionary. The Vietnam War thrust its bloody hand into our living rooms. We saw images of men walking on the moon. Too quickly, the deep-rooted traditions that sustained Sayville and thousands of other American communities became the "pleasantly retro" artifacts of a faded world. Suddenly, upward mobility, be it white collar, blue collar, minority, or women, demanded lateral mobility, a willingness to relocate continuously over the course of a career.

I've made a life a thousand miles from my hometown with my wife, a woman whose family's career migrations carried her from Sewickley, Pennsylvania, to Ohio, Wisconsin, Connecticut, and New Jersey. Our daughter has left for college; our son will soon follow. Both, perhaps, will choose to live elsewhere.

There is a downside to this mobility. Today's America is essentially an anonymous society, a nation of 281 million strangers. Studies suggest *that in some areas of the country, 15 percent of the population pulls up stakes each year—a 100 percent turnover every six or seven years. Millions more, great numbers of them illegal aliens, cross our porous borders, their names, intentions, and whereabouts for the most part unknown. In the 1980s more than one million farming families left the land, never to return. Small-town life, the reality and the myth, has faded. In the new America, a land of bulldozers and raw earth, freshly built tract housing and planned communities, you can barely keep track of your next-door neighbors, barely know the man who fixes your furnace, works in the next office, delivers groceries or installs the satellite dish. You don't know the teenager who tutors your child; the football player dating your daughter; the nanny who spends hours alone with your toddlers. Once these were neighbors, church members, and referrals passed around by family and friends, but that circle has been broken. So you are forced to assume, or you innocently assume that the stranger who comes to your door means well. Mostly you're correct in assessing these risks. Sometimes you go terribly wrong.*

The America of small towns and familiar neighbors has vanished. There is much to mourn in its passing and much to recommend moving on. But there is no doubt that a void exists where once there was the fullness of community, an emptiness that must be filled if our nation is to remain a haven in a world once again shadowed by violence, chaos, and anarchy.

Over the years, I've come to believe the way to protect society is to restore the very best of small-town life. I'm not recommending a vast exodus from the cities and suburbs, or, on a larger scale, a retreat from the global stage. I use "small town" symbolically, but my words are grounded in fact. The risks associated with the revolutionary changes of the past forty years have not gone away. Threats are coming faster and faster. All-too-often they are sped by technology.

And so it is technology, responsibly used, that can rekindle the sense of community, security and safety that defined small-town life. Technology that can be used to reduce the dangers shadowing our lives, livelihoods, and our nation. I'm not referring to security systems and electronic fences, but to information technology. Powerful new technologies are already being marshaled to protect us from enemies who would subvert so much that is good and positive into chaos and anarchy.

PART I

TODAY'S UNCERTAIN WORLD

The world has become a riskier place to live, work and do business. At the dawn of the twenty-first century, Americans awoke to find themselves in a world of unimagined risk where fanatics penetrated our borders, determined to destroy our institutions and way of life. We watched dumbstruck as their murderous cruelty was cheered and echoed across parts of the developing world. At home, a new breed of criminals began to stalk our children across the Internet. Other predators, cloaked by the very anonymity and mobility of our society, were drawn to our schools, houses of worship, youth clubs, and volunteer organizations. In the boardrooms of companies well-known and obscure, executives violated every tenet of responsible behavior, taking a piece of our innocence along with the jobs, life savings, and pensions of thousands of employees and investors.

The common denominator in all of these newly realized risks: people. Oftentimes people we thought we knew, or people we assumed were exactly whom they claimed to be—people of good character and intent. Some people we ignored or dismissed as harmless, when in fact they meant us great harm.

Identity itself was proving fragile and inconstant, easy prey to terrorists, thieves, and con men. The threats these people represented seemed to come from everywhere and nowhere; often they were sped by the power and pervasiveness of American technology.

Today we stand on the edge of a battlefield of a wide ranging Risk Revolution. As with all monumental changes in society, none of this happened overnight. The warning signs were there in plain sight, yet we frequently chose to believe that bad things only occurred to other people in other places. We were transfixed by the ending of the Cold War and, closer to home, the sweeping changes that transformed America from a land of small towns and familiar faces to today's highly mobile, essentially anonymous society. We failed to account for the risks inherent in the new world order we helped create. *Risk Revolution* explores the origins, implications, and challenges of this new world of risk.

Change is inevitable, often positive, sometimes unforeseen and unimagined in consequence. Technology, particularly information and knowledge technology, has driven many of the changes. It will continue to play a powerful role in shaping our lives and potentially, the survival of our nation. However, technology is impartial and can be used for good or ill. The same technological advances that allow us to travel, communicate, or move assets rapidly across the globe, enable our enemies to move swiftly and secretly against us. On September 11th our own airliners were turned into weapons of mass destruction. The 1995 Oklahoma City bombing made it clear that the same fertilizer that nourishes the land can be used to scorch the earth.

The path to a safer, more secure society leads, at least in part, to the responsible use of three of today's most powerful new people-and-relationship identification technologies: data-analytics, biometrics, and forensic DNA analysis. There are powerful lessons to be learned in the discussion of their origins, implementation in real world situations, and potential future applications.

If enemies conspire against us under the cloak of anonymity or false representation, data-analytic technology can find the hidden links that can identify terrorist or criminal conspiracies. It can "see" the associations between people intent on fraud and deception in a way the human brain cannot. Combine analytics with the latest advances in data sharing which are far more appropriate for government use than the centralized information warehouses of the business world, and you have an information system that reduces risk while protecting privacy.

If identity—today anchored by driver's license data and Social Security numbers—is under assault, then biometrics provide an opportunity to shore up the society's fundamental building blocks of identification through technology. These tools are highly accurate and specifically designed for the consensual use of information in applications as people seek privileges from society.

And if those people who seek to do harm avoid creating a paper or electronic footprint in society, DNA identification technology can help point out the telltale presence and identity of a criminal. It can enhance justice by trying to avoid convicting the innocent, but freeing the wrongly accused when it happens. DNA also helps bring closure to a victim's grieving family when ordinary identification is impossible.

These are immensely complicated scientific advances with equally complex social policy implications. It's imperative we put a human face on what all too often is considered the cold and faceless machinery of the Information Age. To point out there is comfort to be found in the knowledge that crimes are being solved, conspiracies thwarted, predators taken off the streets, our children protected. It's important that we experience these benefits firsthand to equip us to take part in the decisions to be made ahead.

Precisely because information technologies have the power to protect or potentially violate individual rights and democratic principles, it's absolutely vital that they be used responsibly. To that end, society needs a construct—"Decision Rules"—guides to when information should be used, how, and by whom. Only when we add more formality to the current, often chaotic scheme of information use, will we realize the real value of technology-based tools to society.

All of the issues surrounding increased security are discussed here against a backdrop of increased concerns about privacy, balanced against society's need to identify people who would do us harm. These are (or at least should be) complementary rather than mutually exclusive issues. The time has come to resolve the privacy "debate," to correct misunderstandings, discard labels, and reconcile differences. Just as on a playground when children position themselves on the end of a seesaw to find the balancing point, too much weight on the extremes leads to the breaking point or rigid immobility, not the balance that was sought.

The same result could be in our future as advocates position themselves on the extremes of safety and security issues. The forces of criminality, chaos, and intolerance make no distinctions and have no qualms in their crusade to destroy or cripple our society. There must be a national dialogue on privacy, technology, and security issues, and it must come sooner rather than later. In the aftermath of another mass casualty attack, individual rights may well be trampled in the scramble to tighten security and safeguard the nation. History teaches us that in times of crisis—from the Civil War to the citizen profiling of modern times—we almost always chose civil defense over civil liberty. We can, and must, have both.

The Risk Revolution poses challenges for all of us, irrespective of our roles in society. Foremost among these challenges is the shift of responsibility for risk reduction from the government to businesses, organizations, and even individuals. For the foreseeable future, our state and national leadership is, and must remain, focused on big-picture threats—the pursuit of the snipers who terrorized the Washington, D.C. area in the fall of 2002 and combating nuclear proliferation are clear examples.

But for individuals, taking personal responsibility for managing the risks in everyday life is more important than ever. A generation ago, society—symbolized in this case by the cop on the beat in our towns and neighborhoods—could protect the majority of its citizens from threats that were well-defined and defensible. Today, much of the personal risk we face is asymmetric, unexpected, unpredictable, coming from all sides, often beyond the reach of law enforcement and other governmental agencies. Think of the Scout leader or coach who is later revealed as a child molester or the sexual predator who stalks children, more often than not, across the vast World Wide Web.

Each of us must shoulder much of the day-to-day responsibility for shielding ourselves, our businesses, and our families from harm. Here again, existing information technology can inform and empower us; it can identify and keep evildoers from our doors, daycare centers, workplaces, and places of worship.

Unfortunately, what's still missing is *understanding* and *commitment*. Those two words resonate far beyond our borders. They speak to huge gaps in philosophy, policy, and international understanding. There is a limit to what technology can accomplish in terms of safety and security. The Risk Revolution will not be quelled by technology's magic bullet. Technology cannot undo the rage or despair in men's hearts. Technology alone cannot ease poverty, dispel misunderstanding, or prejudice—the root causes of much of the escalating risk in the world today. If anything, man has blindly unleashed the information storm and it is men, not machines, who hold the fate of the world in uncertain hands.

It is said that a little revolution every now and then can be a good thing. Indeed, we talk about periods of great advances in civilization as the Industrial Revolution or the Information Revolution. We call new products we buy for our homes and businesses "revolutionary." The birth of a free society often comes through a struggle we term a revolution. Revolutions can also be bloody affairs, marked by intense conflict and painful, uncertain resolution. They are many times unsuccessful.

The final outcome of the Risk Revolution has not yet been decided. There is time to influence the course of events that will shape our nation and society at large, but only if we engage the issues before us. The chapters that follow examine not only the reality of risk, but the acceleration of the forces that lead to danger.

CHAPTER 1

An Uneasy Nation

Despite the billions of dollars spent on homeland security initiatives since September 11th, we are still uneasy. When we board an airplane, the person across the aisle remains a source of fear. We react, 281 million strong, to threats made by men hiding in caves and deserts on the other side of the planet. We are stunned at the horror of snipers slaughtering innocents outside restaurants and shopping malls along the Eastern Seaboard, men whose motives remain unknown. Convicted, Andrew Malvo and John Muhammad, stare at us from newsmagazine photographs. We ask ourselves, "What's to keep this from happening again?"

There is no answer. We scan the news eagerly, fearfully, craving certainty, getting none. We've become a stop-light society, our routines cued to colored Homeland Security alerts that say nothing specific, that urge us to secure our homes against biological agents with duct tape. Today, smart bombs and high-tech weaponry cannot shield us against an enemy who operates in tiny cells, able to carry out unpredictable and indefensible attacks.

The sense of well-being and stability, vital to an open society, has begun to leech away. Much happening around us is an anonymous blur. Criminals enter our homes, stalking our children across the faceless expanse of the information highway. Child molesters burrow into the ranks of the very organizations we have trusted to mold and guide our youth. This is the reality of risk. The evidence is everywhere, repeating endlessly like some horror movie loop.

TARGET AMERICA

"True dislike, if not hatred, of America is concentrated in the Muslim nations of the Middle East and in Central Asia, today's areas of greatest conflict."

2002 PEW RESEARCH CENTER *GLOBAL ATTITUDES SURVEY*

Sixty years passed before September 11th displaced December 7th (the day Japan attacked Pearl Harbor) as America's "Day of Infamy." It seems that, like Rip Van Winkle, we were asleep for the last decade. Aware perhaps, but unresponsive to cataclysmic pressures building all around us. Our dreams were troubled by incidents like the hostage-taking in Iran and the barbarity of the "Blackhawk Down" incident in Somalia, but on we slept until that bright September morning. Awake, we are confounded to discover that the United States has come to represent the "Great Satan" to much of the world.

Our leaders mirror the rest of us. They have been slow to comprehend, slow to react to the fact that this animosity is more than chanting mobs in Pakistan or denunciations in the United Nation's

General Assembly, and much more difficult to defuse. Globalization is the new reality. And, for better or worse, we are subject to the forces it has unleashed.

We've ignored the fact that in much of the world, risk is a constant. In much of the world, the identity card, the security checkpoint, the armed escort is a fact of life. The United States, the richest, most powerful, most envied society in history, is, in many ways, the most naive.

We're still grounded in the small town ethos, where there were few strangers and little evil intent. Looking back, it may have been idyllic, but the world, the sphere that stretched beyond snug harbors and familiar horizons, was dangerous. The West was locked in a Cold War against "godless communism." Armored divisions were at the ready across Europe. ICBMs slept lightly in their silos under Kansas's cornfields. Soviet Premier Nikita Khrushchev banged his shoe at the United Nations and threatened to bury us. We deployed atomic weapons in Iran and Turkey. The Russians countered, slipping nuclear warheads into Cuba. The brinkmanship escalated until the superpowers stood staring at each other across the chasm of mutual assured destruction. The human race survived. In fact, a significant percentage of it prospered in a world held hostage to the two superpowers who had achieved, in that curious phrase, "a balance of terror."

Rather than making the world safe, the Soviet Union's fall destabilized much of Eastern Europe, Africa, the Middle East, and Asia. The end of the superpower standoff unleashed religious and political insurgencies, fueled ancient animosities. The United States, imagining itself a model for emerging nations, became their target instead. Mutual assured destruction gave way to "asymmetric warfare," guerilla actions waged by small, scattered cells of determined individuals, loyal to no nation state, who attack, disappear, and reconfigure, frustrating the best efforts of conventional forces.

Like cancer, risk metastasizes slowly. Warning signs are often ignored. September 11th cannot have been a surprise. For eighteen years, the United States had deluded itself, convinced it was immune to events unfolding and animosities building a world away, imagining perhaps, that as the sole remaining superpower, we could walk away from issues and events that were confounding or intractable . . . that we could pick and chose our battles.

Instead we were chosen. September 11th was the culmination of a cycle of violence that began in April 1983 when Islamic bombers blew up the U.S. Embassy in Beirut. Seventeen Americans were killed. Six months later, a suicide bomber committed another more horrendous attack, an assault that would be duplicated in the attack on United Nations headquarters in Iraq twenty years later. He drove an explosives-laden truck into a barracks and, in one fell swoop, killed 241 U.S. Marines.

The mayhem continued through the 1980s. A bomb hidden on Pan Am Flight 103 exploded over Lockerbie, Scotland, in December 1988, killing 278 passengers—payback we're to believe, for an American bombing raid over Libya in 1986. And in the 1990s, more assults. The first World Trade Center attack came in February 1993, killing six and injuring more than a thousand. Nineteen Americans perished in the June 1996 bombing of the Khobar Towers, a housing complex in Dhahran, Saudi Arabia. Five hundred others were injured. In 1998, Al-Qaeda attacks on American embassies in Kenya and Tanzania claimed 224 lives. In October 2000, a suicide attack on the U.S. Navy cruiser *Cole* as it lay at anchor in Yemen killed seventeen U.S. sailors.

The May 2003 bombings in Riyadh and Casablanca, the insurgencies in Afghanistan and Iraq indicate the cycle has not run its course. Risk continues to escalate. In September 2003, reports surfaced that Osama bin Laden was still at work preparing to launch a biological attack against the United States—an attack, by the way, inconceivable in the worst moments of the U.S.-Soviet standoff.

"THE WORLD IS NOT A HAPPY PLACE"

The misgivings many Americans feel about the future are grounded in fact. In December 2002, The Pew Research Center for the People and the Press published the *Global Attitudes Survey,* an assessment of economic, political, religious, and cultural opinions in forty-four countries. Based upon interviews with 38,000 individuals, the report is a cascade of unsettling news for the West—and the United States in particular. Instead of the dream of democracy, human dignity, peace, and prosperity, there is despair. The developing world is bitter, angry, a tinderbox for terrorism. "The world is not a happy place," reads the summary statement. "At a time when trade and technology have linked the world more closely than ever before, almost all national publics view the fortunes of the world as drifting downward."

In the survey, religious/ethnic violence and fears of nuclear proliferation, ranked second and third in a list of humanity's most dire problems. Only the spread of contagious disease (a foreshadowing of the 2003 SARS epidemic) placed higher. The report may prove to be a road map of events to come: sizable percentages of the population in Muslim countries (73 percent in Lebanon, 33 percent in Pakistan, 27 percent in Indonesia) considered suicide bombings and terror directed against civilians "justified" in defense of Islam.

Well before the invasion of Iraq, the image of the United States had been tarnished among longtime NATO allies like France and Germany, in eastern Europe, the former Soviet Union, and most dramatically, in Islamic societies. (In 2023, Muslims in the Middle East, Africa, and Asia will total 30 percent of the world's population.) In Egypt, the recipient of billions of dollars in U.S. aid, a scant 6 percent of the population views the United States favorably. Visceral, man-in-the-street animosity is not only directed at American foreign policy, but American business practices, the spread of our customs and ideas, and, as the survey notes, "American-style democracy" itself.

None of this is surprising. What's troubling is our blindness to what is unfolding and the absence of effective countermeasures and responses. In Africa and the Middle East, the afterbirth of colonialism, repressive regimes, and misguided attempts at nation building have left democracy stillborn, institutionalized terror, and made enemies of faceless, hopeless multitudes we have never met. We are engaged militarily and politically in global conflict, a "brushfire" war, driven not by economics or political ideologies, but cultural and religious exigencies, issues as inscrutable to the average American as the script of the Koran or the Dead Sea Scrolls.

The nature of our democracy leaves us vulnerable. Our adversaries, willing to die for their causes, understand how easy it is to penetrate our defenses. The September 11th hijackers exploited the trust America has always extended to visitors, claiming to be students and tourists. They obtained driver's licenses, rented apartments, bought cars with ease bordering on contempt. They opened dozens of bank accounts—fourteen at one Florida institution—though none had a valid Social Security number. Two of them, eluding a federal alert for more than a year, roamed freely around the country. When the FBI finally issued an all-points bulletin late in August 2001, the alert was not flashed to airport security personnel. Gambling casinos are protected by more stringent security. A stolen credit card triggers more widespread alarm.

America has been targeted by an enemy bent, not on conquest

or hegemony, but on our destruction. The reasons are complex, a mix of economic, religious, historical, and sociological forces, but the outcome is simple: they will destroy or cripple our society, or we will wake up to the reality of this risk and respond, as we've responded to crises in the past, by mobilizing our resources and national will. This isn't the time to examine or assign blame and responsibility. There is so much second-guessing about whether or not the September 11th attacks could have been prevented, but the life and death question is whether we can stop the next assault. Like the ancient Romans we cannot afford to hesitate while the barbarians gather at the gate.

ACCELERATED RISK

The ultimate risk is paralysis. Mike Kami, a friend and mentor, argues that the rapid social and technological changes of the last decades have created such enormous stresses that individuals and societies have begun to devolve and disintegrate. The continuing chaos triggered by the 1991 dissolution of the Soviet Union is one example; Islamic fundamentalism clearly another. Kami, formerly chief strategic planner for IBM and Xerox in their super-growth years, suggests technology has literally accelerated past the ability of the human mind to comprehend it, triggering to varying degrees, a kind of madness that plays out as paranoia and psychotic violence.

"For 8,000 years humans walked at 3 mph," says Kami. "Then 1,700 years before Christ, we discovered the horse which moved about 10 mph. That horse lasted 3,500 years until the steam locomotive came along at 30 mph. Over the last 100 years, automobiles accelerated past 100 mph, airplanes broke the sound barrier, the space shuttle orbits at

24,000 mph, but genetically we're the same as the ancient Egyptians who built the pyramids. This imbalance creates a gap, and in that gap lie fear, hate and insecurity."

In this country, uncertainty is understandable. Fear has birthed powerful, well-meaning lobbies that proclaim themselves defenders of freedom, personal privacy, and individual rights. They ward off, in an endlessly overused phrase, the onslaught of Big Brother. It's not Big Brother who wants to destroy us. Big Brother did not kill innocent people on September 11th. Our enemies are vile and merciless. They are haunted by their own demons, but they harbor no doubts, no hesitation. They want to murder, humiliate, and destroy.

There are still holes in our homeland's security, despite significant structural changes. (We now have a cabinet-level Department of Homeland Security and a Transportation Security Administration. The Immigration and Naturalization Service has been abolished and replaced.) Yet vital issues remain unresolved. We must unite to confront the reality of these risks. We must determine and deploy the right mix of information and other cutting-edge technologies to protect our citizens and our nation. We are at a critical moment in history. We must act decisively or pass into decline and despair.

Terrorism-related risk is the subject of examination and debate in hundreds of books, thousands of articles and reports by experts and veteran analysts. The primary intent of this book is to portray the reality of risk in everyday life—at home, in the workplace, in the context of family and community—and then to examine how (and whether) powerful new developments in information technology are being marshaled to mitigate these risks. Terrorism is part of the picture, but the truth is we're much more likely to be victimized by criminals, child abusers, con artists, and identity thieves and predators stalking us across the Internet.

CHAPTER 2

Criminals in Our Communities and Companies

"If Elizabeth could be taken, it could happen to any of our children. Like September 11th, it has made us realize how vulnerable we are. There is a very real, unseen enemy."

ED AND LOIS SMART

If you've been to Salt Lake City, if you've stood on Main Street and watched the sunrise over the Wasatch mountains or wandered among the rambling houses of the Avenues, with their flower beds and children's bicycles scattered in the front yards, you have found yourself carried on the wings of memory or imagination to small-town America. Maybe it's the mountains that loom over the city like overprotective parents, or the well-scrubbed Mormon missionaries greeting passersby in Temple Square, but the openness, the instinctive trust extended like a handshake to a stranger, is both welcoming and disconcerting. A thing so rare as to be irrelevant in today's world: the belief that everyone means well, and one should do well by them.

So it was no surprise that Ed and Lois Smart, Mormons, parents of six children, allowed the strangers into their home. The first, Richard Albert Ricci, presented himself as a handyman. Unknown to them, he trailed a thirty-year string of felonies that included attempted murder, aggravated robbery, firearms possession, and burglary. The second, a homeless street preacher named Brian David Mitchell, imagined himself the glorious fulfillment of a Mormon religious prophecy. The record, however, would reveal he was a polygamist with a dark history of sexual abuse. It was also no surprise, because predators often repeat their crimes, that Ricci repaid the Smart's kindness by burglarizing their home. He took Lois's jewelry and other valuables. Brian David Mitchell, we now believe, carried off Ed and Lois's most precious possession, their thirteen-year-old daughter, Elizabeth.

At approximately 3:00 A.M. on June 5, 2002, investigators say Mitchell broke into the Smart's rambling home and abducted Elizabeth at gunpoint as her younger sister looked on in terror. Over the ten months that he held Elizabeth, Mitchell inflicted trauma on the Smart family and the people of Salt Lake City that will take years to heal. Against all the odds, Elizabeth was discovered alive and outwardly unhurt. By all accounts, she is well on her way to recovery.

A STRIPPED INNOCENCE

If you visit Salt Lake today, you'll notice a wariness. The real world—September 11th, Elizabeth's abduction, a Winter Olympics staged under the tightest security, the Iraqi war, and the seemingly endless cases of child abuse committed by priests, volunteers, coaches and community workers elsewhere in the county—has stripped away the city's innocence. Like the rest of America, Salt Lake can no longer afford to be a small town.

Americans have awakened slowly to the reality of risk. Historically, we've been shielded by the expanse of ocean and a stable democracy from the cycles of war, revolution, and chaos that have regularly crashed across Europe, Asia, Africa, and the Middle East. The world wars that swept across the twentieth century left the United States homeland physically unscathed. In Korea and Vietnam, the bloodshed took place thousands of miles from home. Until September 11th, there had been no major attack on America's mainland by a foreign enemy for almost 200 years.

Clearly, poverty and the social ills inevitably accompanying poverty have kept the American Dream out of reach for far too many Americans. For the overwhelming majority of us, crime and violence were visited upon the other person, the careless, less fortunate, less privileged person. We clung to that belief in our gated communities and high-rise apartments, in our suburban havens and gentrifying city neighborhoods, in the remnants of our small towns.

That belief was given lie by the sleek BMWs and Mercedes parked by the commuter rail stations of Stamford and New Canaan, Connecticut, on the morning of September 12th. Out of faith or naiveté, those bedrock American traits, we chose to ignore the signs that danger was approaching, chose to keep our heads buried in the sand, or more likely, fixed on the latest round of sports or escapist television, to trust that something awful wouldn't happen to us, or at least not to all of us. No matter what we hear from our political leaders and the media drumbeat, September 11th was not really a surprise. The world had become a risky place long before then. We simply refused to see the signs, or, from my perspective, the telltale information embedded in the data stream flowing around us.

THE CRIMINAL NEXT DOOR

For those who look for the signs of a trend, there was ample evidence of the new reality of risk very close to home. Since 1994, three federal laws—each named in remembrance of a child murdered or abducted and presumed murdered—have been passed authorizing the registration of sexual offenders. The Jacob Wetterling Act offers incentives to states that requires individuals convicted of sex crimes to register with the police after being released from prison. Megan's Law provides for the release of sex offender information to the community. The Federal Bureau of Investigation's national sex offender database was created under the Pam Lychner Sexual Offender Tracking and Identification Act. Each law is a cold reminder of a life lost, a family tragically altered.

At last count, thirty-six states have compiled online sex offender registries intended to shield communities from predators by tracking the whereabouts of these individuals, and in some cases, preventing them from living in close proximity to schools or day-care centers. The courts have upheld the statutes mandating these registries as legal and appropriate.

However, many of these states— Washington, Rhode Island and California among them—have not posted these registries online, because of concerns about ostracism or fears of vigilante action against these offenders. Thus, there are gaping holes in society's ability to track offenders as they move from community to community. In California, more than 30,000 convicted pedophiles, child molesters, rapists, and stalkers have disappeared into the general population after being discharged from prison, probation, or psychiatric counseling programs. Society needs to identify these individuals. Not to harass, brand, or ostracize them, but to shield women and children from violent impulses and fantasies that all verified research suggests are often impossible to suppress.

Make no mistake, driven by strivings they can neither control nor understand, they are out there, seeking out our children. No institution or organization is immune to such predators. In the summer of 2002, California authorities filed sixty-one sexual abuse charges against John Racadio, a known child molester who'd turned up as a Little League team's equipment manager. In Florida, fifty-nine-year old Rabbi Gerald Levy was convicted of prowling Internet chat rooms, seeking nude photos and phone sex from boys as young as thirteen years.

The failure to take seriously these kinds of responsibilities has been catastrophic. In November 2002, the *Seattle Times* reported that a background check of state Department of Social and Health Services employees involved in child-care services, turned up twenty-seven felons, including one individual working in a juvenile corrections institution who'd been convicted of incest and child rape. A *Miami Herald* investigation that year turned up nearly 200 employees of Florida's Department of Children and Families (DCF) with criminal convictions. Among them: child molesters, sex offenders, and drug dealers. Half of them had jobs that brought them into routine contact with children, troubled families, the mentally ill, or the elderly. The uproar over the newspaper stories, which followed other reports that the agency had literally lost track of 1,000 children in its custody, prompted DCF secretary Jerry Regier to authorize mandatory background screening twice a year (using readily available criminal records in Florida's Department of Law Enforcement databases). In the past, the screening had been done every five years. The reforms came too late for a five-year-old named Rilya Wilson, missing and presumed dead. Rilya's is a double tragedy. The child had been rescued from her homeless, crack-addicted mother only to be victimized by the government agency charged with caring for her.

Elizabeth Smart, Rilya Wilson, and other child-victimization outrages we read about on a daily basis still have not eroded the notion that *anonymity* is a right or privilege in a democracy. It is not. New Hampshire's motto—"Live Free or Die"—may be emblazoned on license plates and in the minds of "privacy fundamentalists," but those words were written in 1809. Romanticized as rugged individualism or "Don't tread on me" orneriness, the notion of absolute freedom from scrutiny has always been part of our history. Perhaps it was acceptable, even beneficial, in a nation defined by frontiers and wide-open borders. An America that, like the small town experience, has faded.

The desire to remake, rename, reinvent ourselves . . . to "Go West," leaving all tracks and traces of our past behind, is jarringly out of synch with today's uncertain world. The frontier has passed away. America's enemies are within our gates. Anonymity is a privilege democracy can no longer afford. In the Elizabeth Smart case, a *voluntary* criminal background check run on the Internet from the Smart family's home computer would have pulled up Albert Ricci's felony convictions in seconds. A little more digging would have revealed that the alleged kidnapper, Brian Mitchell, who called himself "Emmanuel," had been accused years before of sexually assaulting his stepdaughter. (With both men, a refusal to authorize the process would have been a warning in itself.) In Mitchell's case, the records would have also revealed a five-year gap in his life, years when he ran up no transactions, had no verifiable address or employment history, left no footprints as he moved through the world.

I believe those who've paid their debt to society should be encouraged, in some cases assisted, in rebuilding lives and careers. Americans' sense of fair play and our democratic and religious traditions encourage forgiveness. But nowhere outside of Greek mythology do we encounter the notion that a society should embrace the sleep of forgetfulness. Information is the only way to mitigate the risk these individuals may represent. They should disclose, in specific situations (e.g., an employment interview or volunteer screening), past transgressions. This is not to force them to wear a "scarlet letter" marking them as evil or unworthy, but to protect the vulnerable—to assure that those charged with determining whether to employ, assign, or delegate responsibilities to these individuals, can make an informed decision, a judgment that can have enormous repercussions on both sides of the table. A youthful mistake never repeated is a positive testimonial. A pattern of negative behavior says something altogether different. Job seekers are often rejected not because of past transgressions, but because they've lied about past transgressions.

Whether you're the owner of a day-care center or a Fortune 500 human resources manager, you must know whether the person you're considering is a convicted embezzler or rapist. Every parent needs to know if the person leading his or her son's Scout troop or directing a daughter's gym class has been found guilty of sexual abuse. Little League teams, church groups, and Scout troops need to know if a predator is hiding behind the mask of coach, priest, or volunteer.

Today, hundreds of thousands of rape kits (biological and other crime scene evidence) are piled in police lockers in cities and towns across the country. Despite the availability of DNA testing (one of the most powerful and promising information technologies), despite the technology's success in identifying rapists and serial killers, despite blistering exposés on *20/20* and *Oprah Winfrey*, the public needs to know that identifiable rapists are still roaming the streets because of funding shortfalls. Ten years after DNA testing became practical, the Department of Justice's Office of Justice Programs, which funds the processing of backlogged DNA samples, was awaiting enabling legislation to move through Congress. Each day's delay keeps thousands of women—our wives, mothers, and daughters—remain in jeopardy.

DANGER ON THE JOB

Given the ever-increasing velocities of the business world, the inability to evaluate or, in the case of e-commerce, even positively identify individuals on whom we are forced to rely has become a dangerous liability. (The General Motors business model where one organization oversees every aspect of production and distribution down to the dealer glad-handing the customer in the car lot is disappearing.) Outside relationships—should they prove flawed or fraudulent—can destroy an organization. On the inside, managers have, relatively speaking, little knowledge of those on whom they rely. Before September 11th, pre-employment screening was typically a "paper in the file" exercise, too often intended to show due diligence in the event of a lawsuit. Things are improving, but until recently, no one was really certain if the driver heading out the gate with a shipment of toxic chemicals was trailing a string of DUIs, if the person in the next office . . . the cafeteria ...working the line was a con artist, convicted felon, or sexual predator. As you're about to learn, in thousands of instances, they are.

The recent plague of corporate-suite scandals engulfing Enron (20,000 employees lost $850 million in retirement funds), Tyco, and WorldCom make the headlines, but unless you were victimized personally, they seem far removed. The real threat is often closer to home.

A few years ago, a check of criminal records, part of a employment screening procedure, indicated that one in four delivery drivers associated with a well-know pizza chain had been incarcerated in the four months prior to the survey. Not charged, ticketed, or issued a summons for speeding or driving with a broken taillight. *Jailed*. A troubling fact, were it known, to millions of parents who without a second thought, allow home-alone children to order-in pizza. That particular risk is being addressed, but it has not been completely rectified.

On September 11th, 2001, 14 percent of airport workers, individuals with routine access to baggage loaded onto airliners, had undisclosed criminal records. This doesn't mean these men and women were security risks or active criminals; it does suggest that, given the heightened awareness of terrorism triggered, for example, by the October 2000 attack on the USS *Cole* in Yemen and the 1998 embassy bombings in Africa, someone should have been looking more closely. An undisclosed criminal history is a red flag. U.S. Department of Justice statistics indicate two out of three convicted felons continue their law-breaking ways. The recidivism rate is in excess of 60 percent.

Let's break this risk down another way: a recent check of 2,000 candidates who had applied for jobs in a nursing home chain turned up 200 with convictions that included murder, manslaughter, and kidnapping. A well-known telecom company screened 1,000 applicants for jobs that entailed having access to consumers' homes. It turned out that 140 of them had been convicted of sexual assault, larceny, home invasion, battery, and other crimes. We've identified these cases. They are certainly troubling, but it is the risk we don't know and cannot mitigate, that is the real threat.

CHAPTER 3

Assault on Personal Identity

Identity is our most personal possession. It can be highly prized, or a measure of shame, embarrassment, guilt, or criminality. An exceedingly complex notion, identity can be defined in ways poetic ("Who am I?") and practical ("Who are you?"). Identity is the interface through which we interact with the world. As such, it should be an anchor. Instead, it is fragile, inconstant, and vulnerable.

Identity theft is difficult to define. Sometimes, it can involve the fraudulent use of another person's credit card; occasionally, the creation of an entirely new entity or persona out of the whole cloth of another life. (Remember the creatures in the film *The Invasion of the Body Snatchers*, who literally took over the physical attributes and community standing of their victims, the ultimate identity theft.) In these cases, the victim may remain unaware for years that he or she "exists" in a kind of parallel universe.

"Someone is using my name and Social Security number to open credit
card accounts. All the accounts are in collections. I had no idea this
was happening until I applied for a mortgage. Because these 'bad'
accounts showed up on my credit report I didn't get the mortgage."

FEDERAL TRADE COMMISSION COMPLAINT

The above consumer complaint was sent to the FTC in 1999. One of
the greatest risks we face can be traced to the fact that identity, a
building block of social order, is crumbling. The very representations of
who we are—our names, addresses, dates of birth, Social Security numbers, and driver's licenses, our academic transcripts and professional
accreditation—are under attack. We live in a society with no gold standard for identity, no unassailable attribute to serve as a touchstone.
Today, more than 750,000 incidents of identity theft occur each year.
Crimes committed by thieves attempting to gain jobs, credit, and cre-
dentials, all the while remaining invisible and anonymous. Unlike
street thugs, these criminals can camouflage themselves in the trap-
pings of respectability.

Often identity theft is used so loosely we fail to register its significance. Time after time in media reports, the offense is portrayed as
financial, an assault on our pocketbooks like a bum check or stolen credit card. (Here are some examples taken from newspaper headlines:
"Hacker Accesses 2.2 Million Credit Cards"; "19 Charged in Identity Theft
That Netted $7 million in Tax Refunds.") In reality, fraud is one of an
array of abuses linked to identity theft. Ultimately, it is a form of counterfeiting. Instead of money or negotiable securities being run off in
quantity, it is *you*. Your defining characteristics are duplicated, reproduced, and scattered among thieves, predators, and worse. They, in turn,
foist the forgery on unsuspecting others, innocents victimized by the
trust and confidence attached to your name.

Over the last two decades, millions of records—birth certificates, Social Security numbers, transcripts, credit card records, marriages, and divorces—were put online with not enough regard for the fact that the information was spilling everywhere, like water in a burst pipe, undirected and uncontrolled. The electronic "pipeline" is not the problem. The problem is society's continuing delay in implementing consistent, coherent standards and guidelines to monitor and protect the flow.

MY GOOD NAME

"Good name in man and woman, dear my lord,
Is the immediate jewel of their souls:
Who steals my purse steals trash; 't is something, nothing;
'T was mine, 't is his, and has been slave to thousands;
But he that filches from me my good name
Robs me of that which not enriches him
And makes me poor indeed."
OTHELLO, ACT iii, SCENE 3—WILLIAM SHAKESPEARE

Identity theft is an aspect of a larger, potentially disastrous issue: *identity itself is under assault.* In simple terms, the set of characteristics society relies upon to definitively recognize or know an individual is no longer accurate or reliable. With disintegration, comes anonymity, a fearsome advantage to the criminal or terrorist. Unchecked, this assault will generate ever more terrible consequences, just as the twenty-year string of murderous attacks on Americans in the Middle East and Africa set the stage for September 11th.

While crime trends downward in most American communities, identity theft (the assumption of the name and/or other "digital representations" of another individual, living or deceased) is accelerating. This is no surprise. A thief with a keyboard and a modem is still a thief. Identity theft is potentially enabled by every insecure transaction we make, every time our names, credit card numbers, or other identifiers are shared or exposed. According to the Federal Trade Commission, in the twelve months beginning September 2003, identity thieves had ripped off nearly 10 million Americans.

At any given time, there may be as many as 23,000 Michael Smiths in the United States, but the digital string (name, Social Security number, driver's license, credit card accounts), like an umbilical cord, is supposed to circumscribe each person as unique. The process tells the world who we are, not personally or existentially, but in a practical way, allowing us to engage the individuals and institutions around us. Credit, for example, once granted by a local merchant on a handshake, is now linked to histories compiled and assessed by credit bureaus and underwritten by computers with little or no human intervention.

Other privileges flow from achievements or documented skills or abilities. Here again identification is critical. A law school diploma coupled with a passing grade on a state bar exam, for example, allows us to practice law. A commercial driver's license proves that we are deemed competent to transport hazardous materials on the nation's roads without inflicting harm on our fellow motorists. A positive credit score tells financial institutions we may be considered good credit risks. Conversely, a criminal history disqualifies us from holding certain positions or may bar us from coming into close contact with children or other vulnerable members of society.

A stolen identity is valuable. Like stock certificates or jewels, it's negotiable and can be used to steal the assets or subvert the privileges of the individual to whom it belongs. It can qualify an imposter for employment or education to the detriment of legitimate applicants.

There are other motivations for identity theft. In some cases, the theft (or creation of a new persona out of whole cloth) is a response to personal failings and insecurities. Not happy with who you are? Embroider a fiction based on another person's standing or achievements. *Catch Me If You Can*, the Steven Spielberg film, is based on a true story. It traces a young man's (Frank Abagnale) attempt to win his father's approval by successfully assuming a string of high profile identities including airline pilot, lawyer, and emergency room doctor. (By the way, such grand theft would be highly unlikely today because of safeguards created by information technology.) In other cases, the identity thief has done things—behaved recklessly or committed criminal acts—that make him accountable to peers and society. He's unwilling to acknowledge or settle that debt.

In the worst cases, in the hands of a sociopath, a stolen identity can rain confusion, financial havoc, physical harm, and emotional distress in waves that ripple across society. The phony identification cards used by underage teens to buy the alcohol that triggers fatal DUI crashes and the masterful passport forgeries for sale in Europe and the Third World are familiar to anyone who surfs the Internet. Like a wolf in sheep's clothing, a fabricated identity can cloak the child molester, serial killer, or a terrorist enabling him to move freely in search of victims.

Four hundred years ago, Shakespeare understood that an attack on identity (an individual's "good name") is devastating. For example, in October 2003, Ivy Johnson, an H&R Block office manager, was sentenced to *six months' home confinement* for stealing the identities of twenty-seven of the tax preparer's clients, destroying her victims' credit, and running up thousands of dollars in fraudulent purchases. Her co-conspirators were sentenced to probation. According to news reports, Johnson was so unrepentant, during her trial she wore a fur to court that she'd charged to one of her victim's accounts. "She got a slap on the wrist for messing with twenty-seven people," said Clio Wilson, a victim's family acquaintance. "That don't make sense."

The identity theft that took place at the White Plains office of H&R Block is particularly troubling because it was a betrayal. Not at the hands of known criminals, but by individuals in whom we've been encouraged to place our trust. Not computer hackers or street criminals vandalizing mail boxes and trash bins for discarded credit card offers. Those H&R Block employees were encouraged by the ease with which technology delivered their victims' assets at their feet. To again paraphrase Shakespeare, this is the unkindest cut of all.

SOCIAL SECURITY NUMBERS— THE DIGITAL DINOSAUR

"The Social Security Administration has been much too loose with its control of Social Security numbers. That's extremely dangerous when criminals and terrorists are able to use Social Security numbers to infiltrate American society."

IOWA SENATOR CHARLES E. GRASSLEY TO *THE NEW YORK TIMES*

For a variety of historic, social, and bureaucratic reasons, the humble Social Security number has become the primary means of establishing identity in the United States, a responsibility it was never intended or designed to bear. As such, it has become a focal point of the assault on identity.

It is helpful to compare the historical concerns and contrasting approaches to identity adopted in Europe and the United States. In Europe—a continent plagued by centuries of war, ethnic strife, and social upheaval, security—neither liberty nor practicality—was the paramount concern. European governments understood that the ability to lock-in identity was fundamental to an orderly society. The intent, all too often, was to suppress rather than encourage democracy, so the internal passport and identity card became the rule.

One of the great democratic triumphs of the American Revolution was the casting off, symbolically and literally, of such controls. "We were founded as a nation with a belief that the ability to move about without having to produce an official identifier was an absolute element of republicanism," says Dr. Alan F. Westin, Columbia University professor emeritus and one of the nation's leading authorities on privacy. "By contrast, in Europe in the eighteenth and nineteenth centuries, you always had to have a passport or a document. If you checked into an inn in England or on the Continent, you produced your papers and the police were told where you were."

As anyone who's traveled abroad understands, that policy remains in effect, whether applied to the college student checking into a hostel, the business traveler in a five-star hotel, or the commuter on a passenger train crossing a border. In Europe, the first thing they ask for is your passport; in the United States, it's your credit card.

So, almost by default, a nine-digit number, created essentially to assist the government in keeping track of retirement benefits, became the standard of identity in the United States. It was not a very high standard, nor was it intended to be, particularly when you consider that Social Security numbers are churned out like lottery tickets. In decades past, it was not unusual for a husband and wife to share a single Social Security number. Or more recently, for the numbers to be used in the transfer of benefits to the children of deceased pensioners.

Today, because it's omnipresent, poorly tracked, and ridiculously vulnerable, the Social Security number cannot safeguard identity. It suffices only because the vast majority of Americans are not attempting to commit crimes. In terms of security, it can serve as trail marker, verifying transactions, detecting fraud, tracing, for example, educational, financial, and employment histories.

The Social Security number has not been replaced (for example, by an identity card embedded with a secure biometric identifier such as a fingerprint) because Americans' historic aversion to internal passports still reverberates across the political and social spectrum, manifested as "privacy concerns" and fears of Big Brother. We've not yet been frightened or motivated enough to act to protect ourselves.

Like so many other risks we face today, the assault on identity is being accelerated by technology. The converse is also true: technology is our best defense against identity theft and other threats. This seeming contradiction is derived from another truth: technology is not inherently good or bad . . . neither the salvation nor the scourge of mankind. Technology is blind. The breakthroughs that enable e-commerce allow the enterprising thief to extend his reach well beyond the mailbox of the widow down the street. Here again, these are not risks inherent in information technology, but rather how immoral or dishonest people are choosing to apply the technology.

According to a study undertaken by Celent Communications, a market research firm, by 2006, a quarter of all identity theft will originate on the Internet—a billion-dollar racket that soon will dwarf the Mafia's best enterprises. Online fraud, the report suggests, is being accelerated, ironic as it sounds, by financial institutions. Many banks and credit card companies have stumbled into the world of e-commerce without putting basic safeguards in place, a shortcoming unimaginable in the brick and mortar banking world. The result, say industry observers, of financial institutions' inability to understand the consequences of their own technologies. A failure in line with

Michael Kami's notion (see chapter 1) that technology always moves much faster than humanity's ability to absorb it.

Unfortunately, Kami's theory does not seem to apply to criminals who always seem one step ahead of honest men. The following case has been cited as a victory in an ongoing Department of Justice crackdown on digital pirates. It's also testimony to the boldness of the pirates and the ease with which they have been able to plunder their victims. Christopher Lee Jones of Pembroke, North Carolina, was indicted for allegedly selling Social Security numbers at auction on e-Bay. An Internet notice posted by Jones was a veritable welcome mat for illegal aliens, criminals, or terrorists:

"100 Social Security Numbers. Obtain False Credit Cards. Identity Theft. I Don't Care. Bid Starts at a Dollar a Piece. USPS Money Orders Only."

I find it amazing that, given the threats society is facing, nothing far-reaching is being done to stem this kind of criminality. In terms of consequences, this is no different from someone hawking guns or drugs. According to the Department of Justice, Mr. Jones has been put out of business, but more than likely he has been replaced by a hundred or a thousand other anonymous con artists, selling versions of the same scheme, but just not foolish enough to advertise on e-Bay.

According to a recent Social Security Administration (SSA) investigation, *tens of thousands* of foreigners are still obtaining Social Security numbers illegally. One in twelve nonresident aliens, according to a report issued by SSA Inspector General James G. Huse, uses bogus documents (visas, green cards, arrival and departure forms) to obtain bona fide Social Security cards. Huse's figures translate to more than 100,000 cards mistakenly issued by the government in 2000. Nor is it speculation to suggest the abuse of Social Security cards goes beyond the stereotype of impoverished workers desperate to obtain medical benefits or employment. The probabilities tell us that at least some of those cards are in the hands of people who mean us harm. "The tragedies of September 11th demonstrate that the misuse of Social Security numbers and identity theft are 'breeder' offenses," Huse wrote, *"with the ability to facilitate crimes beyond our imagination"* (italics added).

Huse also discovered that recommendations for basic antifraud safeguards such as cross-checking Social Security card applications against INS files had never been implemented, despite overwhelming evidence of abuse. In the twelve months after September 11th, nearly nine hundred foreign-born workers were arrested at major U.S. airports for using illegally obtained (not false) Social Security numbers to gain security clearances. At New York's Kennedy and LaGuardia airports, for example, workers holding security clearances were never fingerprinted; their Social Security numbers were not verified; criminal histories went unnoted.

"I JUST STARTED ORDERING DIAMONDS"

Unlike assault and other crimes against persons, which tend to cluster in the inner cities, the assault on identity impacts every segment of society. Examples are commonplace; attempts at solutions widely scattered and often ineffectual. In the spring of 2002, a Tennesseean named James R. Jackson pleaded guilty in Manhattan federal court to twenty-nine counts of identity theft. Jackson's targets of opportunity were corporate executives, men and women traditionally beyond the reach of common criminals.

For an identity thief, the Internet is the great equalizer. It allows him or her to electronically bypass traditional security measures like alarms and security guards. In the Jackson case, it was the victims' elevated social stature (and credit limits) that made them more, not less vulnerable. Jackson testified that with no more difficulty than it takes to buy a book online, he was able to assume the identities of some of the most powerful executives in the country. He then proceeded to ransack their lives.

According to court testimony, Jackson was so confident of his ability to dance away from criminal prosecution, that he continued his scam years after he realized he was under investigation. When finally caught, he agreed, as part of a plea agreement, to describe his modus operandi to a U.S. District Court Judge named Deborah Batts. In an eye-popping round of testimony, Jackson said one of the ways he'd identified his white-shoe targets was by researching *Who's Who in America*. (The evidence indicated the CEOs of Coca-Cola Enterprises and Hilton Hotels were among Jackson's victims.) He'd purchased their Social Security numbers and other personal information (including the "mother's maiden name" used so frequently by financial institutions as a security check) from Internet brokers operating on a no-questions-asked basis.

Stitching together these easily obtained pieces of information into whole cloth, Jackson assumed the identity of each of these powerful men and parlayed the purloined data into convincing telephone scenarios. He used these stories to persuade customer service representatives at major hotels and financial institutions to supply *his new identities'* "misplaced" or "on file" credit card numbers, limits, and expiration dates. Jackson then charged more than $750,000 in jewelry to his victims' accounts, tangling their credit histories in a snarl of missed payments and delinquencies. "I got the credit card numbers," he told the judge. "So I just started ordering diamonds."

More than likely, Jackson is the kind of petty thief who would have never have gotten past the front door of his victims' homes, nevermind access to their financial assets. Technology made a minor criminal a master thief, even a media figure, so much so that he demanded Judge Batts reduce his sentence (he drew eight years and will probably serve less than his full sentence) because he helped alert prosecutors that "the system has certain holes that can easily be exploited."

The holes are indeed gaping. In May 2002, the *New York Times* reported that a group of hackers broke through electronic firewalls and made off with 13,000 credit reports stored in a Ford Motor Credit Corporation database ("a virtual one-stop shop for fraud and identity theft" according to the newspaper). The documents contained, among other things, personal, readily exploitable financial information on men and women living in the most affluent communities in the nation. In another Detroit-area case, an administrator of the Kmart Corporation's stock option plan was indicted for lifting the identity of a retired executive and exercising 176,000 stock options.

In Chicago, Joseph Kalady allegedly stole another man's life hoping to avoid prosecution for his own misdeeds. Secret Service agents investigating a ring counterfeiting birth certificates, Social Security numbers, and driver's licenses, turned up evidence suggesting Kalady had murdered a man named William White in an attempt to steal his identity. A vagrant, White's only significant possession was his name. According to prosecutors, Kalady, about to be indicted on counterfeiting charges, killed White, planned to fake his own death and then attach his identity to White's cremated remains.

The techno-predator is exceedingly difficult to track. Whether a con man, child molester, or terrorist biding his time in a sleeper cell, he must quickly be brought into the light. Information technology can, and I believe must, be marshaled to counter this kind of risk. New analytic technologies can discern and unravel deception; they must be brought to bear quickly. The financial crimes we see today, easily undertaken and exceedingly difficult to thwart, are paradigms for tomorrow's far more devastating assaults.

POROUS BORDERS/CONCRETE RISK

Historically, foreigners seeking to visit, study, work, immigrate, and assimilate into the United States have been welcomed with open arms. In the past, the motives of the asylum-seeker or immigrant were so predictable and nonthreatening, the government often provided these individuals with identities at Ellis Island, rather than vice versa. We prided ourselves in offering the benefits of citizenship to millions of the "huddled masses yearning to breathe free." (Through all the dark days of World War II and the Cold War, no foreigner came ashore to inflict terror and mass casualties on American civilians. A few Japanese mini-subs beached at Pearl Harbor and a handful of Nazi infiltrators were captured on Long Island.) In the 1980s and 1990s, the nation clung to the small-town illusion that no one meant us any harm, even as the risk of terrorism exploded.

All the September 11th terrorists played havoc with identity. Ironically, they used their real names—mocking our ability to trace them—to transfer money, enroll in flight schools, travel, accumulate credit cards and speeding tickets, falsifying documents as they went along. They left "footprints" no one chose to follow. Four of them used fake identification cards to obtain Virginia state driver's licenses in Arlington, a few miles from the White House. They opened thirty-five bank accounts without a single legitimate Social Security number, but no banker chose to question them. In some instances, according to the FBI, they simply filled in random digits on application forms, numbers never checked nor challenged. As a consequence of that particular lapse, hundreds of thousands of dollars used to underwrite the hijackings flowed from Middle East and Europe into the killers' hands. Records of those transactions led to the arrest of their paymaster, Mustapha Ahmed Al-Hawsawi, in Pakistan in March 2003.

BETTING AGAINST THE LAW OF AVERAGES

In this chapter, I've focused on the Social Security number's inability to anchor identity, but every other measure is also failing. Names and addresses are fleeting. A database search will confirm hundreds— maybe thousands—of individuals bearing the same name. The fake ID used by a teenager to purchase alcohol seems trivial until one examines the numbers on youthful DUI's fatal accidents, vehicular homicide, and date rape. Forged green cards, certifying resident alien status and access to a range of privileges are available on the streets of every city. Bogus college degrees are being hawked on the Internet.

The Department of Justice now ranks identity theft one of the fastest growing crimes in the United States. Society's need for laws mandating stiffer penalties for identity thieves has drawn a vigorous, but not necessarily effective, response in Congress.

In January 2003, California Democrat Dianne Feinstein, joined by Republicans Jon Kyl of Arizona, Chuck Grassley of Iowa, Jeff Sessions of Alabama, and Larry Craig of Indiana, co-sponsored S. 153, the Identity Theft Penalty Enhancement Act. The bill, passed by the Senate in March 2003, tacks on additional prison sentences to felonies committed by identity thieves who "knowingly transfer, possess, or use, without lawful authority, a means of identification of another person." In real terms, the law would add an average of two years' prison time to the sentences handed out to identity thieves, not exactly a punishment to strike fear in the hearts of evildoers.

Yet today, the identities of millions of Americans float freely, safe only in the fact that, in a society of 281 million people, the probabilities of one individual being victimized are small. Even that calculus will change. Run the numbers, factor in the exponential compression of time and probability created by technology, and the evil that men are capable of, and the logic and morality of safety in numbers inevitably fails. We may escape, but our children, or their children, will not.

CHAPTER 4

Bad Guys Coming out of the Woodwork

In the summer of 2001, a career FBI agent named Robert Hanssen pleaded guilty to espionage. Among other crimes, Hanssen had been charged with stealing more than 6,000 pages of secret documents, including information that led to the capture and execution of a number of U.S. double agents who had been operating in the Soviet Union during the Cold War. The FBI man didn't betray his country for ideological reasons, the justification used by turncoats as far back as Brutus. The Soviets had plied him with more than $1.4 million in cash and diamonds. Hanssen had continued spying for the Russians after the fall of the Soviet Union, at one point, demanding his masters provide him with a Palm Pilot with wireless Internet capability to better manage his espionage. Hanssen's treachery—he was convicted and sentenced to life in prison—came on the heels of that of another notorious American turncoat, the CIA agent Aldrich Ames. Like Hanssen,

Ames had provided the Soviets with information that led to the execution of KGB agents who'd been working undercover for the CIA.

At first glance, such devastating breaches seem as inconceivable as they were enduring. Together, the two had escaped detection for twenty-four years! These were career men, agents whose actions and states of mind should have been a matter of record, routinely checked. "Nobody was monitoring the buying habits of Hanssen?" wonders Arthur Money, a former Assistant Secretary of Defense for Command, Control Communication, and Intelligence. "If we had been, we'd have immediately detected something screwy. The guy was living way beyond his means." The highly sensitive nature of his job and other aspects of Hanssen's personality—a neurotic mix of sexual deviancy and religious fanaticism—screamed for scrutiny. No one in authority took notice, nor did anyone deploy simple information tools that might have triggered an alarm.

ASYMMETRIC THREATS

America was unprepared for these assaults. We were unprepared on the morning of September 11th, and we may have been unprepared for the unexpected guerilla war that followed the conventional military victory in Iraq in the spring of 2003. This is the new paradigm. Superpower standoffs have devolved into smoldering, debilitating conflicts that cannot be won by decisive battles.

Were we not shocked when Elizabeth Smart's kidnapper turned out to be a man to whom her mother had extended kindness? Are we not stunned by the never-ending series of corporate betrayals? Could 24,000 Enron employees have imagined their leaders would destroy $1 billion in pension funds and send the company spiraling into bankruptcy? Certainly, WorldCom (now MCI) investors could never have foreseen $180 billion in shareholder value wiped out by alleged insider fraud in the *biggest corporate bankruptcy* in history. All of this has unfolded over the last three years.

At first, these seem unrelated misfortunes visited upon an unlucky minority in an increasingly risky world. Yet this seeming randomness veils a new and terrible threat to our citizens, institutions, and interests. Though each example cited above is unique, unconnected by conspiracy, tactics, or objective, they all run counter to traditional notions of risk.

In each case, the threat came from an unexpected quarter. The FBI agent sworn to defend the nation against its enemies becomes a turncoat. Corrupt management teams trample their obligations to employees and shareholders. Foreign "students" unmask themselves as terrorists bent on mass murder. Iraq's defeated conventional army melts into an unconventional force that offsets the advantages of American military power. We're seeing this pattern—*unforeseen risk posed by unimagined adversaries*—proliferating across society.

In military terms, such risk is defined as asymmetric—"a broad and unpredictable spectrum of military, paramilitary, and information operations conducted by nations, organizations, or individual . . . specifically targeting weaknesses and vulnerabilities" (*The Asymmetric Threat*, Michael L. Kolodzie, U.S. Military Academy). Jeff Jonas, founder of Las Vegas based SRD, is seeing information technologies developed to identify criminals preying on casinos also used to identify terrorist conspiracies. He defines the asymmetric threat in familiar terms: "Bad guys coming out of the woodwork from everywhere, reorganizing, recruiting. With no center of power we can see or touch."

Unlike the twentieth century, the defining characteristic of this new century is not the quest for brotherhood, but the reality of risk.

Risk reverberates across every area of our lives. The United States' ascendancy as the sole global superpower has guaranteed neither safety nor security. The clash of competing systems and geopolitical aspirations of the Cold War have given way to religious fanaticism and cultural alienation. Soviet armies have been replaced by adversaries who come out of nowhere, care nothing for their own lives, and have one goal: the destruction of their enemies.

Just months after September 11th, in an act of cruelty that defies analysis or imagining, someone, possibly a rogue American scientist, spread anthrax in Florida, New York, and Washington, D.C. The ensuing panic spread from the halls of Congress to the living rooms and street corners of every American city and town.

WAGING WAR BETWEEN THE SEAMS

At the Pentagon and the war colleges, strategists have long considered asymmetric warfare a strategic and tactical nightmare. In Vietnam, the Vietcong waged hit-and-run guerilla warfare against better equipped, but often slow-to-react U.S soldiers. The Pentagon's favorite slogan—"No one wants to be caught fighting the last war"—seems particularly true.

"Challenging the United States Symmetrically and Asymmetrically" was the topic of debate at a conference at the U.S. Army War College in Carlisle Barracks, Pennsylvania. The most troubling question raised: "Can America be defeated?" The answer, according to military analyst Richard David Steele, who covered the meeting for the *Defense Daily Network,* was "No" in conventional warfare, but an unsettling "Yes" against a patient, determined enemy pursuing an asymmetric strategy.

September 11th was the perfect execution of a fluid, amorphous asymmetric attack. "The political, economic, and technological climate favors an increase in terrorism and asymmetric attack," Steele concluded in his prescient 1998 analysis. "Our enemies will succeed by waging war between the seams. . . ." Asymmetric warfare respects no borders and spares no noncombatants. It targets infrastructure: the public buildings, malls, levees, dams, bridges, power plants, the financial, data, and communications centers that drive the Information Age. And the innocents trapped inside when an attack occurs. It is no coincidence that "soft targets" (as opposed to the "hardened" security of government and military installations) are mentioned in terror alerts and advisories. No coincidence that security around these public sites has been beefed up. No coincidence that the very randomness of these threats has a multiplier effect. Think of the panic and horror spread by John Muhammad and Andrew Malvo who terrorized millions on the Eastern Seaboard, closed schools and emptied malls, cost businesses hundreds of millions in revenue.

Asymmetries are at the heart of an array of economic and personal risk ushered in by the Information Age. As I've mentioned, violent crime is at record lows in most major cities, but technology is adding new risks—in some cases, ceding advantage to the criminal and chaotic. The robber storming, guns blazing, into a bank is giving way to the white collar thief at his computer quietly rifling bank accounts, credit files, and investment portfolios, diverting the assets of others to his own purpose. The gaming industry, long the playground of organized crime, is more concerned about criminals armed with microprocessors and miniature cameras than muscle-bound thugs. In Las Vegas, the high-IQ "MIT gang" has replaced La Cosa Nostra. We warn our children never to talk to strangers and discover they've been victimized by a chat room predator or a rogue priest rotated from one parish to another, his crimes abetted by a church hierarchy that sought to limit the risk of embarrassment, civil liabilities, and criminal prosecution.

Asymmetries lie at the root of the Al-Qaeda threat because America is not driven by fanaticism, mindless resentment, or the willingness to sacrifice its children. "Asymmetries bring surprise," says John Allen Williams, a former Pentagon planner, now a political science professor at Loyola University in Chicago "With the Russians, it was land army versus land army. Today, the enemy is not coming up the middle any more. Al-Qaeda is not running around with spears. They have access to chemical weapons, radios, cell phones, the Internet. They have the technology to penetrate our systems on a very narrow front—cell phones in their caves. Commandeering our airliners got them technology long enough to hit the buildings. The big question is 'Can they get enough advantage in one area for long enough to achieve strategic surprise?' That's how wars have always been won. Bringing your forces to bear at the decisive point at the critical moment."

Like other risk, asymmetries can be offset. The development of sonar and depth charges blunted the ferocity of the U-boats in World War II. Today, as you'll see, information technology becomes the weapon of choice against the rising tide of asymmetries all around us. Unlike the Cold War, the threat is not annihilation, but the slow grinding down of will and spirit, that mix of ability, optimism and decency that has always defined the best of America. "In many ways we are far better off today," adds Williams. "We don't have people ducking and covering and worrying about the whole society being blown away in an afternoon. Terrorists don't have the ability to destroy us as a functioning society. For fifty years, our primary enemy did.

"On the other hand, the threat may be smaller, but it's much more likely. One irony is that democratic processes make it harder for democracies to defend themselves. The thing that makes us worth fighting for makes us vulnerable."

A RISK-AVERSE NATION

For nearly two years after September 11th, the U.S. economy eroded with more velocity than many of the indicators measuring growth or stagnation would have predicted. Stories in the media trumpeting corporate scandal fueled American's distrust of the private sector. Setbacks in Iraq began eroding support for the government's international policies. Like a snowball rolling down a hillside, each of these issues increased concerns over the next, and the next, until it seemed we were afraid to open our newspapers or turn on the television, dreading the latest setback. In many cases, we never noticed the good news.

To me this is evidence that we're becoming a risk-averse nation, driven by an understandable and overwhelming instinct to avoid any more pain, fear, suffering, or anxiety. If this downward spiral accelerates, opportunities will grow scarce, job creation will sag and unemployment rise, demands for infrastructure and social services will not be met. We'll see escalations in crime, the divorce and dropout rates, and, ultimately, social decay. This is the burden of the asymmetric threat. In my experience, now is the first time significant segments of the population are more concerned about preservation than opportunity. We're looking back rather than looking ahead.

This uncertainty is a cousin to the despair that gripped the nation during the Great Depression. It's apparent at every level of endeavor. Among CEOs, more energy is being expended on governance than driving new business and innovation. "The striking difference between now and then," ITG/Hoenig chief economist Robert Barbera told the *New York Times*, "is that the supreme confidence that things would work out has been replaced by a ghoulish fascination with what could go wrong."

The venture capital market, a barometer of economic confidence, began drying up. Young entrepreneurs dreaming of building the next great busines were being turned away. Part of the reason is wariness, but at a deeper level, risk and failure have become intertwined and co-equal.

We're seeing risk-averse behavior across society. In the travel industry, Americans who regularly traveled abroad on holiday are having second thoughts after the horrific attacks directed at Australian and Israeli tourists in Bali and Kenya. Other general anti-American feelings seem to lurk everywhere in the world. College enrollment is declining, particularly in traditionally black colleges, because many young people are no longer convinced of the benefits of higher education. In the spring of 2003, those who did finish school found themselves facing one of the worst job markets in decades. In January 2004, the economic recovery that began late in 2003 had done little to improve job prospects.

Like the ostrich whose head-in-the-sand response to threat makes it more vulnerable, timidity increases our chances of being hurt. It's much too early for a reliable analysis, but the "malaise," the crisis of confidence President Jimmy Carter sensed more than twenty-five years ago, may be finally taking root. In February 2003, when the Department of Homeland Security raised the terror threat level to "orange," millions of us began laying in supplies of food, water, batteries, and duct tape. It was behavior that recalled the bomb shelter paranoia of the 1950s rather than the stouthearted resolve displayed by Americans during World War II. On television, we heard the story of a Connecticut man who'd literally wrapped his house in plastic. Who could fault him?

New asymmetries confront us daily. They must be addressed. As I've mentioned, thousands of convicted sex offenders, ignoring statutes that require them to report their presence to police, have disappeared. They are moving around freely, popping up in unsuspecting communities where inevitably, some will seek new victims. In Seattle, 150 convicted sexual predators, claiming their offender "status" makes them pariahs unable to find jobs or housing, mingle with the teens and tourists gathered in Pioneer Square—an asymmetry created by a law designed to protect the vulnerable.

INFORMATION—THE ULTIMATE WEAPON

"The geographical boundaries of national security have changed. America has become a potential battlefield for major assaults. Yet we have not developed a sophisticated use of information and information technology to protect Americans from attacks at home. Information analysis is the brain of homeland security."

PROTECTING AMERICA'S FREEDOM IN THE INFORMATION AGE
THE MARKLE FOUNDATION TASK FORCE, OCTOBER 2002

Information must be used to offset risk. In today's world, information makes us faster, smarter, and quicker than those who would do us harm. In the past, the oceanic divide and our military prowess kept us safe while much of the world was being destroyed. (The Soviets suffered 20 million casualties in World War II.) In past, the outlaw stayed outside the gate, his ability to wreak havoc curtailed when the lawlessness of the frontier passed into history.

We barely know our neighbors. Our families have scattered. Our relationships often are as fleeting as an instant message. To counter asymmetric risk, technologies must be sped by public/private sector partnerships, the kind that converted factories and assembly lines into the world's most formidable war machine in the 1940s. It can be done. In the winter of 2001, American technology turned asymmetry to advantage: Special Forces soldiers spearheaded the destruction of the

Taliban, the fundamentalist Afghani regime that aided and abetted Osama bin Laden. The Northern Alliance's struggle against the extremists had been deadlocked for years when the Americans arrived with their satellite phones, Internet-enabled laptops, geo-positioning devices, and night-vision equipment. Lasers and infrared devices "painted" entrenched enemy positions for carrier-based pilots who used smart bombs to devastating effect. That deadlock ended in a matter of weeks.

A handful of soldiers armed essentially with information did what would have taken tens or hundreds of thousands of soldiers to accomplish in the past. Our nation is starting to adapt information technologies on the domestic front, but we have a long way to go. We must become more agile, flexible, and mobile. Information is absolutely crucial in ferreting out what the bad guys are up to and rooting them out before they can act.

Arthur Money, currently Chairman of the FBI's Science and Technology Advisory Board, has spent a lifetime dealing with the ebb and flow of threat and counter-threat, insurgency and counterinsurgency. The asymmetries, the anonymous enemies so willing to use technology against us, leave him despairing of our inattention, our seeming inability to react to danger. Money sums up his fears succinctly: "History suggests we don't get through this without another catastrophe."

In the pages ahead, you'll discover that powerful information tools, able to mitigate risk, are now on stream. On a symbolic plane, I believe that technology can restore the certainties of the past; provide the security so many of us drew from small towns and familiar neighbors. It will take tremendous effort to marshal these tools and deploy them responsibly. It will take consensus and fierce determination. But we must go forward because, in the final analysis, indecision in the face of determined enemies is the ultimate asymmetry.

PART II

THE TIES
THAT BIND

Technology is a broad sword: it cuts both ways. The forces of cruelty and chaos, be they criminals, terrorists, or sociopaths, do not hesitate to turn our vaunted technology against us, a truth underscored on September 11th, when men living in caves on the other side of the planet hijacked our sophisticated technology just long enough to do inestimable damage to our nation. Within our gates, each day brings new evidence of technology being twisted by hackers, identity thieves, pornographers, and sexual predators, the foot soldiers of the Risk Revolution.

The good news is that information technology also has the potential to thwart (though never eliminate) these abuses, to protect our lives, families, homes, and businesses. If identity is under assault, what follows is the call to arms needed to ensure we preserve the information foundation of "who" we are. Using real-world examples, we see information's power at work as database technologies, enabled by probable cause, paint a picture of the risky relationships unseen by the human eye—the relationships that quickly become the ties that bind us to our deeds. It is in this new realm of "link analysis" that seemingly disparate strands of data are being harnessed to counter the virulent threats we face.

CHAPTER 5

New Ways of Thinking

Technology is often portrayed in the media, among advocacy groups, and by some politicians as tools more likely to deprive civil rights than protect them. In reality, technology is one of the tools needed to solidify the foundations of our identities as we know them—the increasingly compromised Social Security numbers, dates of birth, and other digital identifies that today give meaning to who we claim to be.

The question then becomes, what technologies offer the best hope for searching for the nuggets of information that provide value to government without violating the rule of unintended consequence by inadvertently creating the surveillance society we all fear? As we move to other forms of nondigital identity, how will we ensure the base information remains viable and available?

It's important to understand the distinctions between what may be appropriate information practices in the business world, and what is a right and proper use by the government. Most commercial information applications involve the use of centralized databases that may include data on a variety of subjects or from several sources, all tied to a common element. This information is, for the most part, voluntarily supplied, and is part of the fuel that has stoked the consumer-driven economy during the past decade.

There is risk, on the other hand, if government agencies begin to compile massive amounts of information in a centralized database. Witness the often justifiable concerns about several government proposals to facilitate information sharing by physically relocating data on millions of Americans in this type of database. Simply put: bigger is not always better.

A much better approach, I believe, is a new, emerging model of information sharing that is based on a so-called "distributed network" model. In a distributed network, data in government files is not "dumped" into a central data warehouse the way it might be in a commercial business application. Instead, technology allows different government agencies to securely share information on an individual query basis when there is an open investigation based on probable cause. For example, local police departments could share information across city or county lines. States could share important law enforcement data with other states or the federal government. All without giving up control over who gets access to specific data for specific investigative purposes.

Many Americans think this occurs today, but it does not. Think back to 9/11 and the criticism of government officials about a lack of information sharing between government agencies. While the will to share information is much better than in 2001, the technology that allows for it is just now becoming mainstream.

As the evidence makes clear, fears about civil liberties being imperiled or destroyed because of information tools are overblown. Our nation is locked in a life and death struggle against terrorists, child abusers, and other criminals, not an academic or philosophical debate. I've argued that all technology has the potential to be used for evil. Certainly, society must make certain these tools are used responsibly. And then we must act. There are tremendous benefits to society waiting for us when we do.

MATCHING TECHNOLOGY WITH NEEDS

Scoring and profiling are statistical techniques used to mitigate risk, most often financial risk. Using a numeric scale, scoring allows a mortgage or credit card company to determine the probability, based on an individual's past history, that she will be responsible in managing her finances. In this approach, risk cannot be eliminated, so it is spread across the population. A good financial manager is assigned a numerically high credit score.

While beneficial when applied appropriately, such statistical analysis is inappropriate when it is used by insurers, for example, to redline property (homes and businesses) in so-called high-risk neighborhoods. The fact, and this is purely an illustrative example, that 50 percent of the individuals living in an inner city area have filed property and casualty claims cannot be used to deny insurance to the remaining 50 percent. This kind of probability analysis is at the heart of racial and ethnic profiling. If 5 percent of the individuals in a given community are committing 50 percent of the crime, it is statistically imprecise and morally wrong to interdict the 95 percent who are completely innocent.

In the security arena, probability analysis fails completely. One suicide bomber making his way into a shopping mall renders the fact that 99 others were stopped, meaningless. Profiling can deflect investigators from following real leads, rather than fact-based senarios.

A better way of assessing risk is the linking of known facts with real people. In simple terms, link analytics is software that is designed to examine public records and other database information to detect connections and nonobvious relationships that may exist among individuals and/or organizations engaged in conspiracy or criminal activity. Typically, this information is scattered among the billions of documents and records (e.g., a change of address) generated in the course of daily life. Sometimes these connections are intentionally hidden links. Analytics is not, as often portrayed in the media, all-powerful, invasive spyware used to probe the details of the everyday lives of ordinary people.

In a more mundane context, link analytics is one of the most effective tools of the Information Age. For example, the Amazon.com computers that examine your purchases, discover your affinity for medical detective novels, and alert you to the newest Patricia Cornwell thriller run a type of analytics program. On a more sophisticated level (and with your permission) the software might put you in touch with other Cornwell fans to facilitate the formation of a book club.

In a security context, let's use the example of the cardsharks and scam artists explored in detail below who descend on Las Vegas casinos. If I'm looking for collusion between card dealers and gamblers, the fact that there's, let's say, a 65 percent probability of a dealer and a gambler knowing each other, doesn't help me. Any action I undertake automatically discriminates against the innocent 35 percent of my customers. It's in my interest to stop *all* these scams; catching most of them potentially puts me in the hole for tens of millions of dollars.

Applying link analytics, once I know an individual on a terrorist watch list has the same phone number as another individual (or that individual's wife's brother) I have a connection. That connection, in turn, can trigger other levels of association, both broad and deep. Armed with this data, I can now turn to more traditional investigative approaches. The connections uncovered by analytics are far more powerful than anything derived from scoring, modeling, or probability analysis.

Importantly, unlike profiling, link analytics operates within a narrow subset of individuals who may represent a known risk. Once probable cause is established, you can begin to expand your search based on the verifiable information that links people. This is a much more efficient than casting a wide net, hoping to catch the small number of people who are actually linked to the risk you seek to mitigate.

It also passes the common sense test: if you are looking for the miniscule percentage of travelers probability tells us are likely to be terrorists and you stop one hundred people at the entrance to the gates of an airline terminal, you're going to have ninety-nine angry and innocent travelers. It's wrong. Society won't accept this. It shouldn't and because of today's technology, it no longer has to.

FIELD OF DREAMS

In the early 1990s, Jeff Jonas arrived in Las Vegas, a town, that draws its share of both dreamers and bad guys. By law, Nevada gambling casinos can have no interaction with known gamblers and other undesirables blacklisted by the Nevada Gaming Commission. Licensing bodies in Atlantic City and other states operate under similar restrictions. "We're required to know who people are," says MGM Mirage senior vice president Alan Feldman. "And, more importantly, to know they are who they say they are."

From the moment Jonas touched a computer keyboard, it was only a matter of time before he realized his dream, software (a type of link analytics engine) that could be used to unravel the complex knots of false documents and bogus Social Security numbers scam artists used to commit fraud. He called his system NORA—Non-Obvious Relationship Analysis.

In simple terms, link analytics systems work by detecting those "hidden" relationships (typically conspiracies) among individuals or organizations. For example, a woman, who wins a car at a Louisiana casino raffle and turns out to be the (differently named) sister of the woman picking the winner. ("An amazing coincidence!" she told the casino security men who showed up at her door.) Or the roulette player at a casino whom surveillance cameras recorded "past-posting" (placing bets after the ball had fallen). Typically, roulette cheaters employ distraction teams to spill drinks, feign arguments, or otherwise draw the dealer's attention as the scam plays out. In this case, the cameras detected no distraction team. Suspicion immediately fell on the dealer as well. Confronted, he shouted his innocence, claiming he'd never seen the cheater before in his life. Link analytics, using the dealer's name as a starting point, made a connection though a shared a phone number. From there, investigators were able to determine the two alleged cheaters were roommates.

Over the years, link analytics sytems have been refined. The software now "scrubs" data, correcting transpositions in spelling or numerals—inadvertent or intentional—of names, street addresses, telephone and Social Security numbers. Some do this in multiple languages, including Urdu, Pashtu, Farsi, and Arabic, in real time. Tapping a database containing the records of 250 million people, queries can map an individual's suspect relationships in less than one second.

Link analytics systems know that there are 100 ways to spell

Mohammed. The software realizes that "Dick," "Dickie," "Richie," and "Ricardo" are all part of the Richard root name. Latitude and longitude are used to find over-the-back-fence connections that would not show up in a street address comparison. The most sophisticated systems undertake entity resolution, an issue that continues to frustrate investigators. "If you detect three people with the same name and one attended an Al-Qaeda training camp, one just rented a moving van, and another has bought a load of fertilizer," says Jonas, "you really need to figure out if they're all one person."

"This is significant stuff," says Chris Tucker, former chief strategic officer for In-Q-Tel, the CIA's venture capital operation. "The really scary part is that its not being implemented fast enough. If there's something being done well out there by commercial vendors for commercial entities, the government should, at a minimum, be implementing the best of it. None of this is really secret. The secret would be if we were not taking advantage of what the private sector is already using."

The next logical evolution of analytics is the development of an anonymization system that, if it works, will safeguard privacy and enhance national security. In simple terms, anonymization allows the comparison and correlation of identity information contained in different databases without the details being shared.

First, identity data would be shared in an anonymous fashion to ensure there is (or is not) a match against the identity information stored in the systems being searched. Only when a match occurs would the actual data be revealed to authorities to establish the probable cause needed to expand a link analysis-based investigation.

Much of this is still theory. There is a logical order to the way a robust link analytics system must be developed and deployed—entity resolution (confirming unique identities) first, then anonymization. Anonymous data sharing without highly accurate entity resolution could have the opposite effect of failing to detect risky relationships. Likewise, resolved identities are more valuable and versatile when they can be used in a way that furthers the cause of increased safety *and* preserving privacy, the goal of the next generation of anonymization technology.

I believe we will succeed in creating such a system, one that results in a probable cause–based information sharing process for government that mirrors the permission-based system that exists today in the business world. That is a technologist's dream that will be a reality.

CHAPTER 6

Fatal Connections

In the last week of August 2001, Nawaf Alhazmi and Khalid Al-Midhar purchased business-class tickets on American Airlines Flight 77, departing Washington, D.C. for Los Angeles at 8:10 A.M. on September 11th. Both men were on a terrorist watch list after being spotted at an Al-Qaeda summit in Kuala Lumpur in January 2000. They bought tickets using their own names. No alarms sounded. Majed Moqed purchased a ticket that week using Al-Midhar's frequent flier number. A fourth man, Hani Hanjour, used Al-Midhar's address to book his seat on Flight 77. Salem Alhazmi made a reservation using an address matching that of his brother Nawaf Alhazmi. All five were onboard when the Boeing 757 smashed into the Pentagon.

Had the technology to track such a catastrophic risk been clearly authorized, vital evidence might have been developed in the months before September 11th to stop the attack. It turned out that

Al-Midhar's address was identical to that of two other hijackers, Mohamed Atta and Marwarn Al-Shehhi, who flew American Airlines Flight 11 and United Airlines Flight 175 into the North and South Towers of the World Trade Center. A search of Atta's phone records would have yielded five other hijackers: Mohand Alshehri and Fayez Ahmed (United 175), Wail Alshehri, Waleed Alshehri, and Abdulaziz Alomari (American 11). Wail Alshehri also shared a P.O. box with Flight 11 hijacker, Satam Al Suqami.

On August 29, Ahmed Alghamdi, who was on an INS watch list, reserved a one-way ticket on United 175 departing Newark for San Francisco. The address on Alghamdi's reservation matched that used by his brother, Hamza Alghamdi, when he booked passage on Flight 175. Hamza lived with Saeed Alghamdi, Ahmed Alhaznawi, and Ahmed Alnami who were on board United Airlines Flight 93 when it crashed in Pennslyvania. The fourth United 93 hijacker, Ziad Jarrahi, had shared an address with Ahmed Alhaznawi.

UNRAVELING CONNECTIONS

These fatal connections stretch in all directions like the strands of a spider's web. Nawaf Alhazmi shared bank accounts with three other hijackers. Atta used his credit card to purchase plane tickets for two others. Other conspirators, part of Al-Qaeda cells in the United Arab Emirates and Hamburg, Germany, wired the terrorists $500,000 much of it deposited in bank accounts in Florida. There were other links to the now-familiar flight schools; a man once believed to be the "20th hijacker," Zacharias Moussaoui; and a March 1999 tip from German intelligence to the CIA identifying Marwarn Al-Shehhi as a threat.

Using Nawaf Alhazmi and Khalid Al-Midhar as a starting point, link analytics, could have unraveled these connections in seconds, sending alarm bells clanging at the FBI and CIA. At United and American Airlines' ticket counters in Boston, Washington, and Newark, alerts would have flashed on computer terminals. Not one of the 19 would have been allowed near an airliner. Instead, our nation suffered the greatest tragedy in its history.

BIRTHING A NEW TECHNOLOGY

These powerful tools did not appear out of nowhere. They evolved, enabled by the aggregation and integration (putting together and connecting) of databases into enormous information streams. In the 1990s, that process—made possible by the computerization and warehousing of public records, credit reports, educational, employment, and other documents in the 1980s—expanded exponentially. Dramatic improvements in processing speed, storage capacities, standardization, and most importantly, connectivity, allowed databased information to be accessed logically and efficiently.

In turn, these databases were overseen by "gatekeepers" (similar to operators who control the dams and locks on a river), who apply rules and guidelines governing the legitimate flow of information to other warehouses, creating immensely powerful and predictive networks.

Twenty-five years ago, such systems were as unimaginable as space travel to citizens of Victorian England. Criminal records, for example, had to be hand-harvested, photocopied, or in some cases, handwritten in the course of visits to courthouses around the country. Ten years ago, the Internet became a pipeline through which data (aggregated on CDs, tapes, and across high-speed telephone lines) could be distributed. The flow increased as bandwidth (the diameter of the "pipe") continued to expand. Proprietary and personal information flowing through these channels is typically encrypted to safeguard it. It must pass through "gateways" which authenticate, certify, and verify its accuracy.

To sum up, the first wave of the information technology revolution digitized information. The second introduced systems that formatted, secured, and standardized information, allowing databases to "talk" to each other and make "apples to apples" comparisons.

Unlike goods trucked into a warehouse (logged in and stored as inventory awaiting distribution), information flowing into databases can be understood as living records, unique histories of events, transactions, and achievements. A birth certificate, a marriage license, a law degree, a property deed, an employment history are some examples. Hard copies of documents are not warehoused; it is information taken from them—accessed with permission and protected by stringent safeguards—that's aggregated. Because we're dealing with individual human lives, information tells stories: a death, a divorce, a property sale or foreclosure, a career switch. Sometimes documents include physical descriptors; for example, height, weight, and eye color recorded on a driver's license.

One level deeper, this information reveals other things. Airline records recreate travel histories. If there is a higher purpose in analytic technology, it's the fact that when sifted, combined, compared, or contrasted, data yields insights that can be acted upon to reduce risk. For instance, an applicant being considered for a school bus driver position may have an out-of-state history of DUI that would affect his ability to do the job. Another example: it's well known that health-care professionals are hesitant to criticize their peers, even when there's ample evidence suggesting a pattern of error, malpractice, or abuse.

With this in mind, access to malpractice judgments recorded in a database might alert us to the skills or lack of skills of the surgeon scheduled to operate on our child. Similarly, a stream of "slip and fall" insurance claims will certainly factor into an insurance company's willingness to extend coverage to an individual. Credit reports and criminal histories flag potential problems with prospective employees or business associates. None of this is "random" information culled without permission or purpose. Much of it is under regulatory guidelines. Access to predictive information is critically important in a society where people are constantly in motion, continually changing jobs, moving in and out of relationships.

If we go even deeper, it becomes evident that records reveal *connection*. Transactions are not open-ended. A marriage certificate names both bride and groom. An apartment lease may contain the names of roommates. A telephone record identifies both parties. A frequent flier number used by two unrelated individuals making an airline reservation speaks to us. Such an "error" committed by an individual listed on a terrorist watch list should have sounded a loud alarm.

FOOTPRINTS IN THE SAND

We all leave footprints as we move through our lives. We rent an apartment, earn a degree, buy a car, book an airline reservation, install a telephone, and enlist in the military. Each transaction creates a record, a trail, a trace, somewhere. In the world of information, the car you bought and sold in college lives on long after the vehicle is scrap. The college roommate you haven't thought about in years is still linked to you on the lease you both signed. Driver's license applications record our weight and height. An online book purchase triggers a request for a credit card number and a zip code.

Too great a flood of information will wash away meaning. The overwhelming percentage of database information reflects nothing more than the blameless lives of ordinary individuals. Some, however, document connections that, examined in greater detail, may signal criminal behavior or conspiracy. In the deliberately unstructured "dispersed" networks favored by terrorists, connections can represent nodes—hidden command and control structures that enable funding, initiate the transport of deadly weapons, or order an attack.

The challenge is to find meaning in this flood. Link analytics may be understood as a filter that strains this enormous data flow. It recognizes patterns, identifies connections, and uncovers relationships among individuals or organizations that exist at degrees of separation beyond the processing power of the human brain. One degree of separation defines the connection between husband and wife. Discovering that your college roommate's ex-wife's current husband is an U.S. Senator represents four degrees of separation. The conceit of John Guare's play and later movie adaptation, *Six Degrees of Separation*, is that all people on earth are connected by six or fewer relationships. Today's software is powerful enough to detect relationships at up to *thirty degrees of separation*.

A CITY UNDER SEIGE

It is this power to see the ties that bind us to one another that increasingly is the fine line between solution and frustration. Link analysis technology sped the search for the snipers who murdered eleven people in the fall 2002. From September 5th until October 24th, the unknown shooters terrorized the nation's capital and the surrounding suburbs. The big break in the case came when fingerprints lifted from a gun magazine at a murder scene in Montgomery,

Alabama, matched those of Lee Boyd Malvo. That linkage was developed from traditional investigatory procedures. It was slowed, however, because the Montgomery police had never forwarded the murder suspects fingerprints to the FBI's national database.

It turned out that Malvo, who had lived in Antigua as a teenager, originally had his fingerprints taken by Immigration and Naturalization Service agents after an altercation between his mother and a man at a house they shared in Washington State. The man turned out to be John Muhammad. With Malvo identified as a suspect in the Alabama killing, investigators focused on Muhammad, searching databases, which quickly yielded his addresses, marital history, motor vehicle registrations, military, and other records. When database information also confirmed Muhammad's ex-wife, Mildred, lived in Clinton, Maryland, the hunt was on in earnest.

All this data was connected; nothing was random. There were false leads and missteps: the hunt for a nonexistent white van reported by witnesses; the fact that Muhammad had been stopped by police a number of times during the spree and sent on his way; the intolerable delay with the Alabama fingerprint evidence. Humans make mistakes, particularly under intense pressure. What is unmistakable is that information technology helped end the terror.

CHAPTER 7

Solving Crimes

The impact of new analytical technologies leapfrogging into new applications and, in turn, enabling other solutions, is staggering. None of it happened overnight; it began with individuals taking small steps, tinkering, making discoveries, building upon them, priming the pump. Pioneering companies like CDB Infotek in Santa Ana, California, and Database Technologies in Boca Raton, Florida, created systems that could cross-reference names, addresses, employment records, Social Security numbers, dates of birth, telephone numbers, driver's licenses, vehicle registrations, marriage and divorce decrees. In the public and private sector, this information is vital to any number of tasks: verifying titles in real estate transactions, tracking "deadbeat parents" for child support, uniting separated families, locating heirs to estates, witnesses to accidents or crimes, alerting citizens to environmental hazards, identifying doctors with extensive malpractice histories.

The most dramatic breakthroughs have come in criminal prosecutions. Investigations that would take months or years of arduous legwork can now be worked from a desktop, uncovering information about individuals, but also relationships between those individuals and other persons, businesses, and organizations. "In 1987, I taught myself how to use computers," says George Bruder, a former Broward County, Flordia, deputy sheriff. Like many of us, Bruder backed his way into the Information Age. "I had this gun collection which included an AR-15 rifle," he says. "I began studying up on personal computers and wound up trading my rifle for a 286 computer with a printer and modem. It never would have occurred to me at the time, but the computer turned out to be a lot more powerful in combating crime than the assault rifle."

When Bruder began using his computer he and his fellow officers could not access information efficiently. They couldn't tap public information sitting, for example, in files at the Florida Department of Motor Vehicles. They had no quick way of knowing whether someone they'd stopped on a routine traffic violation was an escaped convict, a wanted bank robber, or an ordinary Joe who happened to be in a hurry. A decade later, the September 11th hijackers would run up infractions that never triggered closer scrutiny. Mohamed Atta, one of the leaders of the group, actually abandoned a rented single-engine airplane on a Miami runway and walked away without triggering any red flags.

An investigator who wanted to run a search had to radio a dispatcher, provide a first name, last name, middle initial, race, sex, and date of birth. If any part of that entry, even the middle initial, was incorrect, there was no hit. Often lost time means lost lives. Sooner or later, every detective finds him or herself in a child abduction case involving parents in a bitter custody battle who simply grab their children and disappear. Before linking technologies, these investigations were dependent on "trap and traces" (petitioning phone companies to trap incoming calls to individuals who might be connected to a suspect, then tracing the call back to the originator). Many times, there would be a phone number without a name or address. Often information had to be subpoenaed. In a kidnapping committed by a stranger, every hour that passes increases the likelihood that the child will die.

In those early years, a handful of Florida law enforcement officers determined to push the envelope stumbled across Database Technologies (DBT), a start-up data-aggregating company, and began tapping it as an investigative resource. As the company moved more information online, these searches became faster, deeper, the connections more significant. The first "hits" came on those same child abduction cases detectives find so frustrating. By the 1990s, George Bruder, for example, had begun locating missing children so regularly that the National Center for Missing and Exploited Children (which focuses on the prevention and recovery of abducted, endangered, and sexually exploited children) asked for his help.

Bruder's colleagues, many of whom were still committed to phone and footwork, began paying attention when the technology helped identify a teenage murder victim found alongside a Broward County road. All the investigators had to work with was the date, time, and location of the body—and a single word, "Sara," tattooed on the woman's ankle. It was a case that could take months to piece together. The identification—the victim was a runaway—was made in a matter of hours. Today, DBT's linking technologies are smarter and much more sophisticated. The best part, Bruder says, is that there's still a cop's brain in the middle of the system.

Analytics is a "disruptive technology." It changes everything that has gone before and alters everything to come. Today, no professional criminal, however clever or careful, is able to operate without leaving what law enforcement types call "footprints in the sandbox." He can wipe off bloodstains and fingerprints at a crime scene, put degrees of separation between himself and his confederates, but there's no way to completely erase all the digital evidence of his comings and goings—communications, residences, purchases, travel, and financial transactions. "Analytics is one of the most incredible law enforcement tools out there," says Glenn Kerns, a detective with the Seattle Police Department. "You can't hide from it."

Kerns personally began tinkering with information technology to investigate a surge in street gang crime in his city. The gang members he was dealing with left few paper trails. "These guys had no credit," he says. "They used cash for all their purchases. Their addresses were often mail drops they provided when they needed to make bail." There was one exception to the no-paper rule: "They only thing these guys seemed to do besides buying pizza was rent cars and videos."

While investigating a drive-by shooting, Kerns noticed that witnesses had described the assailants' car as a "four-door, beige sedan." Experience, which goes hand-in-hand with technology, kicked in. "I knew that type of car was the last thing gangsters would drive," he says. "Bingo! A rental." Kerns discovered a database that provided various kinds of practical information to tourists and other consumers. It included one very interesting fact: the name and location of the one car rental agency in Seattle that accepted cash deposits.

He called the agency, described the vehicle and the date of the shooting. He was immediately rewarded with a "hit." The suspect who'd rented the beige sedan had provided the agency with a valid driver's license which allowed the investigation to move forward quickly. The suspect car had been cleaned up, returned and re-rented, but Kerns got luckier still. "We towed it in and our crime lab people found a .45 caliber shell casing in the little trough where the windshield wipers meet the hood," he says. "It matched the gun. We had the guy nailed!"

THE HUNT FOR A SERIAL RAPIST

In a case that has gone largely unnoticed, linking analytics brought down a serial rapist, one of society's most vicious and destructive criminals. In the summer of 1997, a rapist began prowling the streets of the Central City district of Philadelphia. He moved lightly, almost delicately, a contortionist who slipped into women's apartments through balconies and open windows as they slept. His first victim was so paralyzed with terror, she couldn't resist. Emboldened, he broke into another young woman's apartment a few weeks later and choked his victim into unconsciousness before raping her.

Such cases are as commonplace as they are horrible. Philadelphia detectives arriving at the scene logged the second attack as a burglary, blurring a connection that would later prove significant. In both attacks, the assailant left behind genetic evidence (hair and semen-stained underwear) that was collected in a "rape kit." Instead of being analyzed, this evidence was stored in a police locker because neither victim could identify her assailant. As we'll see in a later chapter, the advent of DNA databases for convicted felons has the potential to revolutionize this flawed and inefficient process.

Given the backlog of sexual assault cases involving unknown assailants, many months passed before DNA identification linked the two attacks—and only then because the level of violence had escalated. This is often the case with "opportunistic" criminals. The burglar becomes a rapist; the rapist a murderer. At the time, all the police had to go on was a physical description. As if sensing this, the predator raped two more women. They lived a few blocks apart, an easy walk from the sites of the other attacks. The following spring, he materialized again, this time on the second floor terrace of an apartment building. He slipped through an open sliding glass door, surprising Shannon Schieber, a twenty-three-year-old Wharton business school student at her studies. Unlike the other victims, Schieber fought back.

A neighbor, hearing the struggle, called the police. Officers arrived at the apartment, knocked, and, according to reports later published in the Philadelphia Inquirer, walked away without investigating. Her brother found Schieber's body the following morning. Eight months would pass before DNA analysis, undertaken after the crime, identified Schieber's murderer as the man who'd committed the earlier attacks.

In this case, the assailant's genetic "fingerprint," a string of numbers derived from a unique biological marker, triggered no "cold hit" (identification derived by matching biological evidence against convicted felon DNA databases). By now, composite sketches of the killer were appearing in store windows and bulletin boards in downtown Philadelphia, accompanied by the inevitable panic that accompanies such assaults. In August 1999, the killer attacked still another woman. And then he vanished.

Twenty months passed before the murderer resurfaced—this time 1,500 miles from Philadelphia. In May 2001, a twenty-year-old student was raped in her apartment near the campus of Colorado State University in Fort Collins. A month later, a second woman was brutalized. The third rape triggered panic in what had been an open and trusting college community. A fourth attack took place in July, the fifth in August. The rapist was spiraling out of control, becoming bolder, more reckless, likely to kill again. Just days before September 11, 2001, he attacked two women, this time roommates he encountered in their apartment.

In Seattle, Glen Kerns took notice (Philadelphia detectives had telexed a national alert hoping to generate some traction in the case). The bulletin contained descriptions of the assailant, a timeline, and other details. "I called the Fort Collins detective running the case," Kerns recalls. "I told her 'Databases are my passion. I can help you solve this.' She told me she had 400 suspects and, by the way, she'd already heard from enough psychics."

At that point DNA had implicated Schieber's killer in twelve other assaults. The genetic fingerprints, though tantalizing, could provide no further help. The man they were hunting, one among millions, either had no prior history of sexual assault, or as is often the case, his information had not been taken, analyzed, or entered onto a DNA database. Kerns voluntarily began to work the evidence. Descriptions obtained from victims pegged attacker as between twenty and thirty years of age. His height somewhere around five feet eight inches to six feet.

Kerns began to massage the databases, cross-referencing data, including the dates and zip codes in which the attacks took place. His next step was to put together a list of men of the right age who lived in the cities at the time of the attack. In the past, such needle-in-a-hayfield analysis could take years and produce nothing.

Using custom algorithms, Kerns ran an initial search using Philadelphia five zip codes and males aged twenty to thirty who'd lived either in Philadelphia or the Fort Collins area at the time of the attacks as search elements. The zip codes were important because the evidence fit the profile of a rapist who lived close to the scene of his crimes. That run produced 45,989 possible suspects. Including height and driver's license data narrowed the search, and the number of potential suspects dropped to 825.

The next run tracked men fitting the established criteria who had lived in *both cities at precisely the time the attacks took place.* That list contained just eight possibilities. Duplications reduced the suspects to six. An excited Kerns, who still had no official role in the investigations, got on the phone with Philadelphia detectives. "The lieutenant told me 'I know two of these people! We have them as suspects.'"

One was Troy Graves, born May 4, 1972. An Air Force enlisted man who had lived in Philadelphia, Graves had joined the military two days after the last Philadelphia attack. He'd eventually been transferred to an airbase in Fort Collins in the spring of 2001. His was the first name on Kerns' list.

"We'd narrowed it down to the two they could focus on," he says. "Standard police work solved it from there." Using fingerprint evidence taken from one of the crime scenes as probable cause, Fort Collins police ran a DNA test. It turned up positive, and Graves was subsequently charged with all the assaults. "One page is closed," Vicki Schieber, the mother of the murdered student told a *Philadelphia Inquirer* reporter. "And that is good."

Graves pleaded guilty in the spring of 2002, a plea bargain arrangement that spared him the death penalty. He is now serving life in prison. If there is a deeper tragedy here, it's that the two new information technologies, analytics and DNA analysis, might have been brought to bear sooner. If they had, Schieber and the other victims might have been spared. "The information is always out there," says Glen Kerns. "The question is, 'Will we use it?'"

CHAPTER 8

Enemies Inside Our Gates

In the months after September 11th, Congress and the media focused on breakdowns in intelligence and communications, particularly the failure of our intelligence agencies to share information that possibly might have prevented the attacks. The fact that the CIA, with the assistance of Malaysia's Special Branch, had identified September 11th terrorists Nawaf Alhazmi and Khalid Al-Midhar at an Al-Qaeda summit in Kuala Lumpur, tracked the two to Los Angeles, yet neglected to notify the FBI until days before the hijackings, is a cataclysmic breakdown.

Alhazmi and Al-Midhar lived openly in the United States for nineteen months, opening bank accounts, enrolling in flight schools, smoothing the passage of the rest of the killers. Similarly, the failure of FBI lawyers in Washington to support requests by its Minneapolis field office for a warrant to search the laptop computer of Zacharias Moussaoui (once believed to have been recruited by Al-Qaeda as the twentieth hijacker) left important clues untapped. Moussaoui, a French national of Algerian descent was arrested on immigration charges three weeks before the attacks. He'd aroused the suspicions of instructors at a Minnesota flight school when he allegedly expressed no desire to learn how to takeoff or land jetliners. The Minneapolis agents, who'd tracked Moussaoui to another school in Oklahoma, were never told that their colleagues in Phoenix had alerted Washington to what turned out to be Al-Qaeda operatives taking flight instruction.

WHEEL OF TERROR

It must also be said that information technologies brought to bear after September 11th have helped prevent other attacks. Obviously, this is highly classified information still being sifted by investigators, but imagine the nineteen hijackers arrayed as points on the circumference of a wheel. Their interactions (the nonobvious relationships we've been discussing)—shared addresses, frequent flier numbers, bank accounts, airline ticket purchases—may be visualized as spokes on the wheel. The point where one spoke intersects with a second third or fourth spoke represents connections at varying degrees of separation. What has not been made public is that the circumference of this "wheel of terror" contained more than the original nineteen hijackers—individuals within and beyond the borders of the United States who are being investigated.

Analytics is forward-looking and creates actionable intelligence. It is being deployed to good effect, precisely the way our high-tech "information warriors" were deployed in Afghanistan. In the years after September 11th, news reports, citing government sources, confirmed that scores of men—believed to have trained in Al-Qaeda camps in

Afghanistan—living in the United States were under surveillance in New York, New Jersey, and a number of West Coast cities. How was this information developed? Certainly by traditional investigative techniques and tips from concerned citizens, but also using analytics. "It is inconceivable that the most powerful tool in the information arsenal, available at a desktop, would not play a part in these investigations," says Jeff Jonas.

The concern, reflected in the Department of Homeland Security's warning system regularly being raised from "yellow" (elevated) to "orange" (high), is that the threat has evolved from suicide attacks on centers of power and commerce like the Pentagon and World Trade Center, to schools, amusement parks, shopping malls, and movie theaters.

Many details are classified, but it is interesting, for example, to revisit news reports (*New York Times*, September 3, 2002) describing the arrest of Kerim Sadok Chatty, a Swedish national of Tunisian background. Chatty was arrested at an airport near Stockholm after attempting to board a Ryanair 737 airliner bound for London with a handgun in his carry-on luggage. Swedish prosecutors accused Chatty of "making preparations for hijacking, aviation sabotage, or airport sabotage." Those charges were eventually dropped for lack of evidence, but other facts emerged. In the mid-1990s, according to news reports, he'd attended a South Carolina flight school; he had links to Oussama Kassir, a Swede of Lebanese descent named as an unindicted co-conspirator in a 1999 plot to establish an Al-Qaeda training camp in rural Oregon.

The most dogged law enforcement investigators working phones or canvassing informers and street contacts cannot unearth these kinds of links. The war against terror or the hunt for a sniper, rapist, or serial killer must be waged in real time. As I've said, after-the-fact solutions are, by definition, no solutions at all.

SLEEPER CELLS

In September 2002, six Yemeni-Americans were charged with forming an Al-Qaeda cell in Lackawanna, New York, an upstate community with a large, close-knit Yemeni population. Federal prosecutors revealed the group had received training at an Al-Qaeda camp in Afghanistan in the summer of 2001 and had provided "material support to a foreign terrorist organization."

As teens, these men—Faysal Galab, Sahim Alwan, Yahya Goba, Shafal Mosed, Mukhtar Al-Bakn, and Yasein Taher—had played high-school soccer, cruised the town in cars and motorcycles. At first glance, they seemed like first generation Americans cycling through the "melting pot." Taher had dated a cheerleader and been voted "Friendliest" in the Lackawanna High class of 1996. Not exactly a terrorist profile.

No weapons or explosives were found in their possession. No smoking gun that would positively identify the six as a "sleeper cell," waiting to be activated. In fact, community leaders insisted they were misguided, culturally alienated, but harmless young men caught in a FBI dragnet scooping up all and any Middle Easterners who seemed the least bit suspicious.

The community had been deceived. In November 2002, Kamal Derwish, the Al-Qaeda sympathizer who'd recruited the six, was killed in Yemen by a missile fired from a CIA-operated drone as he traveled with a group of other terrorists. In January 2003, Faysal Galab, pleaded guilty in U.S District Court to contributing funds, goods and services to Osama bin Laden and Al-Qaeda. (Galab testified he'd attended a lecture at the al Farooq camp in Afghanistan, where he'd heard Osama bin Laden brag that "fifty men were on a mission to attack America.") By the end of May, all six had entered guilty pleas, and a seventh conspirator, Jaber Elbaneh, was on the run.

The evidence used to build the government case was developed by painstaking "shoe-leather" investigative work, but it would be naive to assume analytics engines did not distill evidence from the jumble of airline reservations, phone records, passport entries, credit card charges, and other transactions that trailed behind the men.

In the aftermath of September 11th, airlines rushed to reinforce the cockpits of their jetliners against assault. It is likely that the terrorists, who are sophisticated men, had already changed their tactics. In fact, reliable evidence has emerged that a handful of commercial pilots and other airline employees, foreign nationals flying for overseas airlines, were connected by degrees of separation to Al-Qaeda and other Islamic fundamentalist organizations. These are men who may be flying regularly into the United States.

This kind of information should convince Congress as well as the public safety and intelligence communities to add their voices to the chorus of those of us worried that these powerful technologies are not being implemented quickly enough. Today, there are terrorist watch lists linked to airline ticket counter desktops, a great step forward. Unfortunately, freight is still loaded aboard airliners alongside screened passenger baggage without being checked for explosives. Few of the security safeguards authorized by the Transportation Security Administration to protect passenger airliners have been extended to commercial freight carriers. A hijacked 747 freightliner is just as much a weapon of mass destruction as a passenger airliner. Our ports and harbors remain vulnerable to attack. Our security net is stretched far too thin for any of us to feel secure.

"Why this is still happening is a testament to how convoluted the bureaucratic process is in Washington," says a former ranking intelligence official, echoing a lament one hears like the biblical voice crying in the wilderness. "Everybody from the top all the way to the bottom is going, 'This stuff is what we need!' And yet things continue to move at a crawl. The question is, Can we get the technology implemented to find the scary, bad-guy relationships? Ones we should be taking action on right now?"

Until significant action is taken in Washington (and the ever-increasing number of nations facing or continuing to ignore this terrible threat) that question will hang like a pall over all our lives. The powerful information technologies introduced in the next chapters—tools designed to safeguard our families, financial well being, and civil liberties—are ultimately meaningless in a world gripped by lawlessness and terror.

PART III

THE PROMISE
OF BIOMETRICS

A new era is dawning, a time when traditional identifiers will be displaced by unique, quantifiable physical characteristics known as biometrics. DNA is the best known new biometric, but there are others being developed or already deployed. This transition to a new identity anchor is still in its infancy, but I believe it's as inevitable as the progression from the Pony Express to airmail, faxes, and e-mail.

Biometrics are living proof that technology is positively transforming the ways we live, work, and do business. They represent the ultimate evolution of identity, a process that began 3,500 years ago when the Egyptians developed a primitive form of fingerprinting. As with any new technology, the transition from traditional identifiers like names, addresses, driver's licenses and Social Security numbers will be stressful because it's human nature to embrace the commonplace and familiar. But biometric ID systems, because they require physical confirmation, lend themselves to more conscious, consensual exchange of information as individuals seek the privileges of our society.

As we'll see in the chapters that follow, the emergence of biometric technology has been triggered by terrible risks to ourselves and our nation. Risks that, in many cases, can be traced to nothing less than the increasing failure of today's method's of identification.

CHAPTER 9

The One and Only You

Shoppers arriving at the West Seattle Thriftway supermarket in May 2002 were offered a premium that went beyond specials on laundry detergents and pot roast: fingertip shopping. That spring, the store became one of the first outlets in the country to introduce biometrics to consumers. Electronic scanners installed on sixteen checkout lines allowed customers to make purchases by simply placing an index finger on a pad. No plastic, PINs, or checkbooks required. In ten seconds, according to store manager Brian Bixenman, the scanned fingerprint—linked to credit, debit, or other accounts—is converted to a secure thirteen-point digital "map" and matched against an original stored on a secure server. Purchase approved, transaction completed.

A year later, hundreds of Thriftway customers, ranging from families doing weekly grocery shopping to joggers popping in for a quick bottle of Evian, were using the system without a second thought.

Misplaced wallets, time—consuming check—writing rituals were a thing of the past. "I thought it would be the younger, more progressive crowd that understood computers who'd go for it," says customer service manager Patricia Atkins. "But our older customers have really embraced the idea."

What's happening in Seattle . . . in Fresno, California, where fingerscans authenticate purchases at a McDonald's restaurant . . . at Disney World where season ticket holders glide past snaking admissions lines using a two-finger scanner . . . in schools and offices around the country . . . is the democratization of biometrics. It's the first step in society's acceptance of technology that will transform the way we do business, safeguard our privacy, redefine and strengthen identity.

ONE FROM THE MANY

A new era is dawning, a time when names and Social Security numbers will be displaced by unique, quantifiable physical characteristics known as biometrics. For our purposes, biometrics encompass digital photographs, fingerprints, the mapping of distinctive patterns etched on the eye, and the DNA analysis used for identification purposes. Other biometric identifiers include facial and signature recognition systems, even vocal characteristics created by the particular shape of the mouth, larynx, and other speech-related structures.

This transition, spurred by technology (and the risk created by technology), is as inevitable as the progression from the Pony Express to airmail, faxes, and e-mails. A 2002 survey, sponsored by the Department of Justice's Bureau of Justice Statistics, suggested that 5 percent of the American public (some 10 million adults) has provided a measurement for a "computer-matched biometric comparison"—

typically a fingerprint scan. These measurements were taken upon induction into military service, while applying for a job or license, as part of an identification system run by a financial institution, during a criminal justice proceeding. The survey indicated that three quarters of all business travelers reported they were "very" willing to enroll in a fingerscan system like that used by Thriftway if it would streamline airport check-in lines.

Biometrics represent the ultimate evolution of identification, a process that began at least 3,500 years ago when the Egyptians developed a primitive form of fingerprinting. As with any technology, identification systems remain functional, sometimes for centuries, until new demands or unanticipated pressures render them obsolete or unreliable. Today's movement away from traditional identifiers like names, addresses, driver's licenses, and Social Security numbers has been triggered by the risks created by the assault on identity.

As we've seen, the notion of identity developed exceedingly slowly and then deteriorated rapidly. In 1550, Michael Smith was known in his village by his profession—blacksmith. No further identification was needed. Smith was Michael's name as well as a signifier of his profession. In 1950, blacksmithing was in serious decline and the name Smith had proliferated dramatically. Nonetheless, his neighbors could reliably identify Michael Smith's face. The government knew him by the name and Social Security number on his income tax return or his military record.

In 2004, Michael Smith lives in a society of more than 281 million strangers. His name, of itself, no longer implies a known identity. The Internet propels him into routine contact with millions of anonymous individuals, not all of them trustworthy. He is anonymous to them. How can Smith—our everyman—safeguard his interactions with the corporations, governmental agencies, and individuals with whom he interacts on a regular basis? How do *they* quantify the risk, financial and personal, that may be associated with Michael Smith? More than likely, first through an electronic upgrade of fingerprinting, the venerable identification system perfected in the United Kingdom at the end of the nineteenth century. In the near future, our identity may be linked to the distinctive patterns etched on the iris of our eyes or the shape of our hands. Ultimately, it will be grounded in *iDNA**, a numerical representation of the unique structures in the nuclei of our cells. At the moment, technology allowing instantaneous genetic-based identification, so-called "*iDNA* on a chip" has not been perfected.

Today, with fraud and identity theft rampant, with the threat posed by predators and terrorists growing, when information and assets can flash, essentially unguarded, across the globe in seconds, the particular biometric marshaled is less important than the defining aspects of biometric technology: it is *unique* and *consensual*. Each individual, not a government authority or private corporation, plays the vital role in vouchsafing his or her identity. The individual decides, where, when, how often and with whom to share his information.

Our names and birth dates might as well be written on the wind, but we *possess* our biometrics. They're difficult to steal or corrupt, far easier to monitor than our digital identity. There are thousands of Michael Smiths in the United States today, but distinctive "grooves, whorls and ridges" mark each Michael Smith's fingerprint as unique. In a fingerprint-based biometric system, stealing Smith's identity requires nothing less than a duplicate of the patterns etched on his finger. This is different and much more difficult than filching his VISA card from his wallet or buying a purloined Social Security number on the Internet. A criminal may create multiple aliases, but he only has one

---

* To avoid confusion over the various terms—"DNA sample," "genetic fingerprint," "forensic DNA," "genetic signature"—used almost interchangeably by the media and law enforcement and often misunderstood by the public, I've used the term *iDNA*, to refer to an identification system-based on unique strings of numbers derived from human DNA sampling.

set of fingerprints.

Michael Smith's *iDNA* is unique and distinguishable from the billions of humans on earth today. It can survive cataclysmic events like airplane crashes and the World Trade Center attacks. It will identify him centuries after his death.

RESTORING TRUST, ONE FINGER AT A TIME

The Department of Justice's study cited above was the first national survey of Americans' attitudes toward biometrics. Undertaken by nationally known privacy experts Alan Westin and Robert Belair, the study indicated electronic fingerprints, retinal scans, and other biometrics are viewed as tools that, used responsibly, can reduce personal risk and make society safer. It also reported that half the U.S. population is more or less familiar with the term "biometrics." Of those, 82 percent believe that every adult will have a biometric identifier on file by 2010. The Americans already enrolled on biometric registers say they are comfortable doing so. Substantial numbers voice support for the use of biometrics in antiterrorism, intelligence-gathering, and criminal investigations.

According to Westin and Belair, nine out ten Americans favor embedding biometrics in the passports or visas of foreigners seeking to enter the country, a standard recently approved by the federal government. Eighty-five percent accept the use of biometrics to control access to government buildings or screen passengers at airport check-in counters. An unexpected seventy percent have no problem running facial scans at sporting and civic events to winnow out criminals; eighty-five percent support running the biometrics of motorists stopped for traffic infractions against a criminal database.

It must also be noted that eighty-eight percent say they are uneasy "about the possible misuse of personal information." People demand safeguards against unauthorized government and private sector abuses, and they want to be "fully informed" about the use to which their biometrics will be put. Specifically, they want assurances that personal data will be protected (using encryption or other secure technologies) and not shared unless required by law or expressly authorized. Concern over biometric abuse runs deeper than that of other forms of identity theft. Unlike a driver's license, a stolen biometric (converted in these systems to a string of numbers or a mathematical "map") cannot be reissued.

A Harris poll conducted shortly after September 11th indicated that sixty-eight percent of the American population favored "a national ID system for all Americans," a number that flies in the face of our historical insistence on freedom from government intrusion. To be effective, such a system would undoubtedly be built around a wallet-sized card containing embedded biometrics, most likely fingerprints and photographs. That percentage may have eroded somewhat in the past few years, but it's certain to rebound in the aftermath of another terrorist attack. Gut instincts are often right. It's important to remember how devastated and helpless we felt in those terrible days. That memory should force us to seek and demand responsible ways to reduce risk.

These surveys reflect the mood as well as the insecurities of the post-September 11th world. To me, they suggest Americans want to restore the sense of normalcy and security that is bleeding out of our lives, including, as far as possible, the right to be left alone. As one skeptic of a national identity card program put it, "No one wants to live in a world where you put your finger down somewhere and someone has access to your whole life." Incidentally, that was one of the significant concerns expressed by Thriftway customers in Seattle. The good news, according to store managers, customers, and cash register operators, is that security safeguards—carefully explained and implemented—went a long way in allaying any Big Brother paranoia.

CHAPTER 10

Life in the Fast Lane

In the next few years, biometric systems will become more sophisticated, practical and user-friendly. (At the moment, the idea of staring into a retinal scanner while a device measures the distinctive pattern of the blood vessels of one's eye is unsettling.) There are competing technologies and in all honesty, no efficient "one-to-many" application capable of expanding the Thriftway model into a system able to reliably identify one individual among tens of millions of otherwise unknown users. What does exist are "purpose cards" encrypted with biometric information that boost speed and efficacy of the verification process.

A successful biometric implementation will not depend solely on legislation, but built-in safeguards and demonstrable efficiencies. Smaller ("closed") systems will become common. Fingerprint scanning systems will oversee access to computer networks, office buildings, and college libraries. Over time, there will be a tipping point, much like there was with e-mail, fax machines, and debit cards, when a significant segment of the population suddenly realizes, "Wow, it's in my best interest to get one of these!"

This tipping point will come sooner or later. In the worst case, it will follow another catastrophic attack. In this scenario (unfortunately, quite plausible), the intense security imposed in the aftermath of such an event will leave people on the streets fighting for entry to their own offices and shops. Underpaid, poorly trained security guards will attempt to search and check everyone, echoing the chaos that crippled U.S. commercial air travel for days after September 11th. Worse yet, they will undoubtedly rely on driver's licenses—as we've seen, an "identifier" completely vulnerable to fraud, duplication, and other abuse.

Those two-hour lines at the airport were reduced only after the government spent tens of millions of dollars to hire and train 50,000 new baggage screeners and several hundred million dollars more on high-tech bomb-sniffing equipment, effectively turning every airport in the country into a security checkpoint. That's impossible in most public areas without dramatically circumscribing freedom and shutting down commerce. The New York City subway system, for example, has as many potential "security checkpoints" (public entrances) as all the airports in the country. There are also the shopping malls, restaurants, office buildings, stadiums, ports, and piers—an endless critical infrastructure that is vulnerable.

VOLUNTARY PRESCREENING

In my view, the simplest and most effective way to mitigate this risk is to let people *designate themselves* low risk. Here the approach is not primarily to catch bad guys moving through the system, but to expedite the rights and privileges of the overwhelming majority of good guys who pose no threat to their neighbors or society. How would that work? A viable approach is to prescreen individuals voluntarily, employing the identification credentialing systems now available. For example, once it's established that a *particular* Michael Smith exists and that the individual enrolling is this unique Michael Smith, his biometric is taken. In this case, a photo, fingerprint, or some combination of the two. If Michael Smith meets predetermined criteria (e.g., he has no prior felony convictions or suspect connections to individuals on watch lists) he is issued a card allowing "fast lane" privileges. This approach leaves security personnel free to focus on those who may represent a higher risk or who prefer not to go through a credentialing process.

No one with legitimate purpose is denied access, though some, flagged by predetermined "decision rules" will receive more scrutiny than others will. Since the system is designed to expedite access and not track movement, no data would be kept on who passes through what portals. Those who abuse this trust for example by, using enrollees' data for purposes for which it was not intended would be subject to civil and criminal penalties.

In my view, the government does not necessarily issue the rules; it endorses generally accepted consensual standards. The authority to set rules and criteria used to establish rights and privileges should, in most cases, reside with the entity accountable for the risks involved. If the owner of an office tower is legally liable for the actions of those who gain entry, then he or she should determine what standards are prudent.

Creating the kind of purpose cards described above is an example of what technology can support. To Americans who regard unrestricted access and freedom as a birthright, it may seem harsh or prejudicial to some individuals. The answer is the United States is not the safe haven it once was. That reality is triggering any number of new security measures across society, granted not all of them effective. Nonetheless, corporations that once took a casual approach to screening job applicants for criminal histories now see that task as vital. Workers in day-care centers are being vetted regularly, along with coaches, teachers and, volunteers. We live in a litigious society. Airline executives or the owners of sports venues, for example, understand they may be held accountable for the security breach that allows a known criminal or terrorist to pass through unchecked. Liability will create some arbitrary decisions in a society searching for security. We cannot avoid these decisions, but we can understand and prepare ourselves to deal with them.

"The people who operate stadiums, shopping malls, and office buildings are starting to think about security," says Steven Brill, the journalist whose *After: How America Confronted the September 12 Era* examined the government and private sector response to the terrorist attacks. "They're spending money, but not on anything that is, in any way, secure. What they're doing now will pale against what they're going to have to do tomorrow morning if there's another attack." Brill has founded a start-up company, Verified Identity Pass Inc., to develop a voluntary biometric identity system based on electronic fingerprint technology.

PERMISSION GRANTED

Reducing risk requires a leap of faith. An acceptance that the small town is gone . . . that neighbors can no longer vouch for familiar faces. It sounds insensitive, but we must credential people just as we have to credential financial transactions. (Of course, using different standards.) In the financial world, if the great majority of borrowers make good on their debt, a lending institution prospers. In the world of security, apprehending 99 percent of the terrorists or child molesters is meaningless if someone manages to blow up a building or abuse an innocent. How do we accomplish this?

I envision *consensual* biometric identification systems (like the ones described above) tied to an assessment of an individual's risk. For the overwhelming number of Americans, tourists, or foreign students, this "assessed risk" will approach zero. From there, it will be a matter of time until public demand, efficiencies of scale, and entrepreneurial ingenuity combine these identification cards with others, like a driver's license or credit card. This is not the same process that creates a *mandatory* identity card. The individual decides whether or not to share his or her information, a determination based on benefits gained rather than mandated obligations.

CHAPTER 11

The Power to Protect

Fingerprint scanning is reliable, cost-effective and nonintrusive. Today's electronic systems are descendants of the ink and paper kits used to investigate crimes and develop evidence against criminals. A whiff of criminal association still clings to the technology, the reason many of us still avoid the inkpots at bank teller counters. What is less familiar is the protective power of fingerprinting. Certainly, it exonerates the innocent in criminal proceedings, but there is more. According to a 2002 report on biometrics that appeared in *Privacy & American Business*, children's medical records at Columbus Children's Hospital in Ohio are protected by a biometric system requiring employees to sign onto the hospital's database using a secure and easily traceable fingerscan. In November 2002, Florida's Supreme Court justices (exasperated by forgotten passwords as well as security concerns) ordered administrators, install encrypted fingerprint scan systems on six hundred courthouse computers.

BIOMETRIC MAPS

These electronic readers scan fingertip "minutiae" (grooves, whorls, forks, and ridges) unique to each person, then input a *representation* of that information into a closed system seeking a match. One version of the technology measures tiny electrical currents across the finger to create a map; another detects miniscule gradations in temperature. Neither system stores nor transmits literal images of fingerprints, something those of us who worry about thieves intercepting data passing between the scanner and database find unacceptable. Algorithms mark a series of data points on a fingerprint, then create a mathematical "map" that is transmitted and stored. It is impossible to recreate the fingerprint from these maps.

Critics claim fingerprint scanning is flawed, vulnerable to attack by identity thieves. For example, the Japanese researcher Tsutomo Matsumoto reportedly used a gelatin "finger" upon which a set of fingerprints was "engraved" and was able to trick eleven different scanners. A group of German journalists fooled another system using residual fingerprints left on the lens of the scanner by a prior user. These challenges are welcome developments. In my view, they serve ultimately, to force improvements in the technology.

No technology is perfect in its infancy. The key to success is constant and consistent improvement in reliability and functionality at a pace fast enough to keep opposition forces from killing or subverting the technology before its value can be proven. This is especially true of technologies that rely on features other than fingers.

The retina, the layer of the eye that receives and transmits images, and the iris, the muscular membrane that controls the size of the pupil, have characteristics that are quantifiable and unique to each person. *Iris scanners* measure the complex patterns nature etches on the iris; retinal systems record the distinctive arrangement of blood vessels inside the eye. As with fingerscans, both techniques register, digitize, and then match an individual's data against information stored in a database.

These systems, though accurate and reliable, are considered inconvenient and impractical. Imagine a situation where large numbers of people are moving through an airport security checkpoint. Each person scanned must sit still—think ophthalmology exam—and focus on a specific point while the data is being read. Imagine doing this while young children wander off and impatient travelers mill around you. In controlled applications (a major defense contractor has deployed iris-scan systems to secure its work areas) they are very effective.

Another biometric system, *hand geometry*, quantifies the unique characteristics of the human hand (contour, the "lifelines" read by fortune tellers, finger length and size, the pattern of blood vessels on the back of the hand). It is most effective in situations where access control and reliability is primary. The best current examples are prisons where guards, are constantly moving in and out of cellblocks. Obviously pass cards or keys would be vulnerable.

Signature and voice recognition systems are "behavioral biometrics," which are grounded in deliberate actions by the individual being identified. Neither is as precise as fingerprint or retinal scanning, though manufacturers declare claim signature systems can detect fakes produced by the best professional forgers. Signature systems require special pads resembling those used to sign off on credit card purchases in department stores—only more sophisticated—capturing the speed, sequence, and pressure an individual brings to bear signing her name.

Voice recognition is grounded in algorithms that recognize the unique vocal characteristics created by the shape and structure of an individual's mouth, nasal cavities, vocal cords, and other speech-related structures. The brokerage firm, Charles Schwab, allows California investors to access accounts via telephone voice-scan analysis.

THE MYTH OF THE BIOMETRICS "REVOLUTION"

All these biometrics systems are evolutionary. They will gain traction from incremental technological advances, a logical, step-by-step implementation that will allow the public to grow comfortable with the new technology. This long-term approach stands in contrast to the stampede of corporations touting biometric "solutions" that took place in the fall of 2001, an ill-conceived rush for sales and government funding that turned into a setback for those of us who understand the real promise of the technology.

The helplessness all of us felt after September 11th triggered a desire for easy answers and quick solutions. It is hardly surprising that the vision of a powerful biometric shield deployed against terrorists grabbed the attention of the media, law enforcement, and national security communities. Many of the companies involved in biometric research came forward with exaggerated promises about the capabilities or readiness of their products. (In all fairness, they were joined by every purveyor of security apparatus, from armored cars and analytics to police band radios and biohazard sensors.)

On the surface, the most impressive technology rolled out was a "one-to-many" facial recognition system that employed video cameras to scan the throngs at airport security checkpoints. Software analyzed and compared distinctive features—eyes, chins, noses, eyebrows, etc.—of the captured images against a database containing photographs of individuals on federal watch lists. The system operated on a scoring system: x number of facial characteristics, out of y number being scanned, equaled a match.

The problem was it didn't work well in this particular application, triggering a backlash just as strong as the fear that prematurely boosted the technology's capabilities. The key to long success is not giving up on the technology, but rather working to make the system better. The efficacy of facial recognition and other biometric identification systems can be determined with two statements: "I win if I'm able to spot Michael Smith in a crowd, but I'm not disadvantaged if I miss Michael Smith." The second statement is fraught with risk: "I may find Michael Jones in a crowd, but not finding Michael Smith can have terrible consequences."

In Las Vegas casinos, a facial recognition system scans blacklisted cardsharks as they come through the door. It's a closed system with a finite number of both guests and con men. Police in Tampa, Florida, deployed facial recognition technology during the run-up to Super Bowl XXXV and later in the Ybor City entertainment district, hoping to identity and prevent known criminals from preying on tourists. Results were disappointinq and the system was dismantled.

In those instances, the stakes were dramatically lower than, for example, at an airport. Boston's Logan, Providence's T.F. Green, and Palm Beach International airports tested facial recognition systems without much success. In Vegas, a "black book" containing photos of known criminals already existed, so incorporating these images into a database was no monumental challenge. An occasional wise guy slipping through the net was not catastrophic. Criminals have money, not mass murder on their minds.

No such all-encompassing database exists for terrorists. Today's facial recognition systems require good lighting and a face-on image of the person being scanned, unlikely in the crowds and tumult of a major airport. Slight changes in facial geometry may fool these systems. A beard, mustache, or even sagging jowl could trigger a false negative. Jackie Fenn, a technology analyst at Gartner, the Stamford, Connecticut–based research and consulting firm, says she was able to defeat the systems in trials by simply puffing out her cheeks. "At Logan airport, the system worked about 20 percent of the time," says Rick Charles, a security and management consultant who heads the Aviation Studies Program at Georgia State University. "If you put on sunglasses, things just turned upside down."

Like the rush of well-being felt when we first glimpsed National Guard troops patrolling our airports, the biometric buzz faded. The promise is real, the technological advances dramatic, but, at the moment, facial recognition systems are neither effective nor practical in ensuring the security of a public place. "After September 11th, companies selling these systems made claims that were above and beyond their true capabilities," says one researcher heavily involved in biometrics. "We're having a difficult time shaking that perception. With additional testing, we're getting a better understanding of how these technologies perform in real-world environments."

CHAPTER 12

Securing
Our Borders

"In the twenty-first century border security can no longer be a coast-
line, or a line on the ground between two nations. It is also a line of
information in a computer. ... In the twenty-first century, it is not
enough to place inspectors at our ports of entry to monitor the flow of
goods and people. We must also have a virtual border that operates far
beyond the land border of the United States."

ASA HUTCHINSON, DEPARTMENT OF HOMELAND SECURITY

With those words, Homeland Security undersecretary Asa Hutchinson
announced the federal government's most wide-ranging biometric initiative: an attempt the close the gaping holes in our borders that have
allowed millions of foreigners to overstay or otherwise violate the
terms of their visas. All too often aliens arriving on work permits or
student or tourist visas simply disappear, untracked and untraceable.

Hutchinson's initiative, dubbed "U.S. Visitor and Immigration Status Information Technology", adds biometrics to the mix of programs designed to address that problem. As of January 1, 2004, foreigners— some 23 million annually—entering the United States from countries where visas are required must provide immigration officials with two biometric identifiers (fingerprints and photographs) as part of the visa process. As the technology becomes more reliable, iris scans and facial recognition systems may be deployed. Congress has mandated that visitors arriving from the twenty-eight so-called "visa waiver" countries must have passports embedded with biometric identifiers.

WHO'S HERE?

Biometric tools will be part of a tracking system allowing authorities to monitor, for example, the terms and length of a visitor's stay. They will provide a basis for verifying departures and identity cross-checks. The INS (dissolved and reconstituted as part of the Department of Homeland Security's Border and Transportation Security directorate in 2003) had no means of tracking foreigners. DHS compliance teams will investigate breaches and enforce the laws against undocumented people. How troublesome is the problem? As I write these words, 3,000 foreign students supposedly attending American educational institutions have officially disappeared.

In the next few years, the system is designed to extend beyond U.S. ports of entry. Overseas, DHS teams and State Department staffers will "confirm identity, measure security risks, and assess the legitimacy of travel of visitors to the U.S." The system, Hutchinson said, would be dynamic—able to track changes in status and input updates and adjustments.

Over the last decade, *6 million* Border Crossing Cards containing biometric data were issued to Canadian, Mexican, and other foreign nationals who travel to United States on a routine basis. The INS never provided the training and equipment to allow Border Patrol officers to decode the cards. "We now have an opportunity to learn from past mistakes," said Hutchinson. "We must not miss this chance."

IN DEFENSE OF PRIVACY AND IDENTITY

Privacy advocates want laws spelling out protections against biometric abuse. Jane Black, writing in *Business Week* called for a "biometric bill of rights" governing the scope, access, storage, and segregation of biometric data. At the moment, there is no comprehensive legislation on the books, but we must proceed with caution. An initiative, fueled by angst or distrust, may shut down or dramatically restrict the information flow, a self-defeating approach.

In my view, an individual should have the right to opt out, i.e., retrieve his biometric, under most circumstances when voluntarily offered. Unlike a nuclear power plant, ringed by concrete and steel, identity is fragile and exceedingly difficult to defend. We've seen names, addresses, and driver's licenses compromised, stolen, or forged. As of 2004, 42 million Americans of all ages, education, and income levels had been victimized by identity-linked fraud, ranging from stolen credit cards to attacks on their savings, investment, and retirement accounts.

We've seen these are asymmetric threats, posed by enemies who understand more clearly than we do, the opportunities for creating havoc in a lightning-fast world. We've watched our digits, the building blocks of our identity, float freely in the ozone of the Information Age.

We understand that in our daily lives, we leave traces of ourselves in hundreds of places. Legitimately, routinely, part of the endless information exchange that allows us to conduct financial transactions, purchase online movie tickets, pay electric bills, travel, or sign an apartment lease.

We're coming to the realization that we don't know, and until recently, couldn't control, what happens to our data—where it goes, who sees it, whether it's repackaged and resold. Each iteration slips further and further beyond our control. Most important, we should realize that since the government cannot protect us, we must protect ourselves. In the small towns of past generations few outside one's family had access to this personal information—perhaps the family doctor, the banker, or insurance agent, maybe the grocer with whom we kept a running tab. Families kept what were once called "important papers" (typically deeds, baptismal and birth certificates) in safe deposit boxes, protected by the hardened steel of a bank vault. Today, the information in those documents is virtual. What was once locked away is out there. And it's everywhere.

It's vital that each of us reconstructs that small-town security vault. In doing so, biometrics becomes a building block that can be used to blunt the assault on identity. As I've said, we choose if, when, and to whom we grant access to our credit histories, educational transcripts, professional licenses, and other personal data. Control reduces risk by guaranteeing you, and not some pretender, is granted the benefits commensurate with your standing and achievements.

Unrelieved, the tension over who accesses and disseminates information will lead to paralysis. Not the familiar Washington gridlock over funding and partisan politics, but capitulation in the face of evil. There's a refrain I've heard from law enforcement and politicians—that today's catastrophic terrorist attack will speed tomorrow's passage of tougher antiterrorism laws. Waiting for another September 11th before we spring to action is too high a price to pay.

PART IV

THE DNA REVOLUTION

In the past decade, DNA analysis has emerged as one of the most potent weapons in information technology's arsenal to combat the assault on identity. DNA-based identification has closed seemingly insoluble crimes, identified and interdicted predators, brought justice and closure to victims and their families. It's being marshaled to reopen criminal cases and exonerate the unjustly convicted, including innocent individuals who've languished on death rows for more than a decade.

Someday, I believe DNA will become the absolute anchor of identity because our *iDNA* often proves our presence when other footprints in society fail or are absent. But, like the strands of James Watson's famed double helix, DNA analysis raises extremely complex questions both scientific and ethical.

The cost of DNA processing today is extreme. Tomorrow, as costs inevitably decrease, *iDNA* use may be as common as the plastic driver's license you carry today. Or, society may reserve *iDNA* for only those cases which represent the greatest opportunity for risk reduction. In either case (or the miles of ground in between) society will decide the degree to which *iDNA* becomes the ultimate identifier.

Ahead, the milestones in the development of this revolutionary technology are examined, as well as its ongoing, real-world applications. And, some of the world's leading forensic DNA experts discuss safeguards that must be in place to ensure that the deployment of DNA technology proceeds with minimal risk and maximum responsibility.

CHAPTER 13

"We Could Have Stopped Him"

In the spring of 1993, a career criminal named Isaac Jones was paroled onto the streets of New York City. Convicted of sodomy in 1983 and robbery in 1989, Jones, age thirty-three, was one of tens of thousands of felons moving in and out of the police precincts, courthouses, and jails of what had become a revolving door justice system. U.S. Department of Justice statistics suggested Jones' years of incarceration guaranteed two things: he would return to the Bronx a hardened predator, and would, almost certainly, commit a new round of assaults. No statistic, however, could have quantified the magnitude of the risk Jones posed to society.

At that moment, the state of Virginia was pioneering one of the most dramatic breakthroughs in law enforcement history. In 1989, the state had set up the nation's first DNA databank. The *iDNA** of

---

* Once the original samples are processed and discarded, the stored numbers are simply digits. They can serve no other purpose but identification. The use of *iDNA* analysis, for example, to predict genetic predisposition to disease is technologically impossible.

thousands of sex offenders were logged into the database. A year later, the Virginia legislature expanded the database to include samples from all convicted felons. Things began to happen. When the database profiles were compared with *iDNA* processed from rape kits and biological evidence from other unsolved crimes, there was a trickle of cold hits identifying assailants in investigations that had been stalled for years. In 1998, the state, facing a backlog of 200,000 collected but still unprocessed samples, began outsourcing the analysis to the Bode Technology Group, a private lab in northern Virginia. As the state database continued to expand, the trickle became a torrent and then a flood.

Other states quickly followed Virginia's lead. Unlike the technology, which is precise, the systems, set up in fits and starts, left many holes in the net. Despite his earlier sexual assault conviction, Isaac Jones' identification profile was never logged into New York's database. (He was one of many felons who fell between the cracks as the systems came online.) Within weeks of his parole, he'd attacked a Bronx woman. In the next six years, he would commit more than fifty sexual assaults in Manhattan, the Bronx, and Westchester County. Jones' long rampage left thousands of women afraid to leave their homes or walk the streets of their neighborhoods. Over time, it inflamed tensions between police and inner city residents who felt that not enough was being done to protect them.

Jones was eventually captured when his wife tried to pawn the jewelry of one of his victims. He was tried, convicted and sentenced to three hundred years in prison. Bronx Superior Court Judge Joseph Fisch, who presided over the first of Jones' trials, said the spree illustrated how one "brutal creature without remorse, contrition, or regret could destroy lives, uproot homes, and traumatize an entire community."

By then, Mayor Rudolph Giuliani and Howard Safir, New York City's police commissioner, had committed millions of dollars to implement a DNA identification program. Unfortunately, New York's database, like those of so many other states, still lagged behind the criminal curve. "Isaac Jones represents a tragedy that did not have to happen," Safir says today. "We had so many samples from the victims. If we'd had Jones' *iDNA* on record, we'd have stopped him after the first attack."

Over the past fifteen years, *iDNA* analysis has become one of the most potent weapons in information technology's arsenal. DNA-based identification has closed seemingly unsolvable crimes, identified and interdicted predators, brought justice and closure to victims and their families. It is being marshaled to reopen criminal cases and exonerate the unjustly convicted, including some individuals who've languished in prisons and on death rows for more than a decade.

In December 2002, DNA evidence fueled a dramatic turnabout in the 1989 horrific assault and rape of Trisha Meili, the Central Park jogger, one of the most contentious and racially charged cases in New York City's history. Five black and Hispanic youths who'd been imprisoned for gang-raping Meili, a twenty-eight year-old investment banker at Salomon Brothers, had their convictions vacated when *iDNA* testing of crime scene evidence confirmed that Matias Reyes, a convicted murderer and serial rapist, had committed the assault.

Equally important, *iDNA* is a forward-looking technology. It can prevent as well as solve crime by identifying wanted criminals before they can inflict further harm on other innocents. It can tear away the veil of anonymity shielding terrorists and sociopaths as they move across our borders, in and out of our neighborhoods, towns, and cities. Today, prevention is the only standard. I can't say this often enough: Solving a murder, a case of child abuse, or a terrorist attack after the fact is not an acceptable outcome.

CHAPTER 14

DNA 101

As previously discussed, DNA identification may be the most familiar example of a new wave of biometrics technologies; unfortunately, it is also the most misunderstood. *iDNA cannot* predict genetic predisposition to disease; it *cannot* be used by insurance companies to discriminate against individuals based on such predisposition. It *cannot* be used to clone a master race or create your genetic double. The technology's great strength is that it can identify individuals at a level of accuracy far beyond that of any other system or technology. Paul Ferrara, who runs Virginia's forensic DNA laboratory, considers the technology so benign he has his twenty-six *iDNA* numbers stamped on his driver's license.

In general terms, DNA (deoxyribonucleic acid) is a genetic blueprint stored inside every cell. Structured in two entwined strands, the famous double helix contains, replicates, and passes on the inherited characteristics of all organisms. The DNA of all human beings on earth is more than 99.9 percent identical. A tiny percentage of the genetic information contained in the nucleus of every cell is distinctive to an individual, even among close family members. As with fingerprints, this uniqueness is the basis of DNA's power as an identifier. Thus, *iDNA* can settle paternity disputes and sort out neonatal mix-ups in hospital maternity wards.

Four chemical compounds (nucleotides) are the building blocks of DNA. These nucleotides (abbreviated *A*, *T*, *G*, and *C*) are the alphabet that make up the genetic code. At certain locations along our DNA, these nucleotides can repeat themselves in clusters like boxcars on a freight train. The number and variation of repetitions (called "short tandem repeats" or STRs) is the basis for DNA identification. The human genome contains billions of individual nucleotides, and thousands of STRs. International standards have been established setting out the particular sites that are used for identification purposes.

In the United States, thirteen STR sites ("loci") on the DNA strand are used for typing purposes. Factor in the number of possible repeats at each of the thirteen sites and the odds of two individuals (excepting identical twins) having the identical pattern is greater than one in a trillion. Put another way, greater than the number of people on earth.

The thirteen sites used for identification purposes are nonfunctional. Spread out among the twenty-three pairs of chromosomes that make up the human genome, they contain no information that could be used, for example, to predict a person's propensity toward debilitating illness or antisocial behavior. The argument—made by those seeking to use emotion to make a case for restricting use of the technology—is that such data can be used to create a class of social outcasts and genetic lepers, or, less dramatically, uninsurables. The reality: *iDNA* databases contain nothing but the twenty-six numbers (thirteen pairs) used to establish identity.

"This string of numbers contains far less data than a Social Security number," says Ferrara. "A Social Security number gives you personal information about somebody—where they were born, where they applied for the card. Getting this message across to people is extremely difficult. When they hear 'DNA profiles,' knowing what they know about Human Genome Project, they immediately think 'All my genetic information!' What they don't realize is that the thirteen core loci we use serve only one purpose: they are far more accurate and immutable than any other method used to establish identity."

Two kinds of DNA are used in forensic analysis. *Nuclear DNA*, as its name suggests, is extracted from the nucleus of cells. *Mitochondrial DNA* is found in tiny, energy-producing structures (mitochondria) scattered throughout a cell's cytoplasm. Both parents contribute genetic traits to nuclear DNA. Mitochondrial DNA is inherited solely from one's mother. There are much greater concentrations of mitochondrial than nuclear DNA in a cell; thus, it stands a better chance of surviving over long periods of time or in the aftermath of catastrophic death. Mitochondrial analysis has been used to extract data from human remains dating back more than 7,000 years.

CHAPTER 15

Cold Hits Bring Justice

By the late 1990s, all fifty states had established convicted-felon *iDNA* databases. In 1994, the federal government passed the DNA Identification Act, establishing standards and authorizing the FBI to create a national *iDNA* database. That database—its acronym is CODIS (Combined DNA Index System)-now contains the genetic signatures of *1.5 million* felons.

Fifteen years after Virginia's breakthrough, *iDNA* technology has become faster, more reliable and sensitive; familiar enough to the public to become the touchstone for Hollywood movies and television series. Thousands of violent crimes have been solved, in many cases piling new convictions on hardened criminals who would otherwise be on the streets hunting new prey. Between 2001 and 2002, nationally, the number of crime scene identification samples registering so-called hits on *iDNA* databases more than doubled to nearly 5,000. By 2004,

Virginia's cold hits alone tallied more than 1,600.

None of this would have happened without the breakthroughs in database technology. The polymerase chain reaction (PCR), a biotech innovation so dramatic it won its inventor, Kary Mullis, the 1993 Nobel Prize for chemistry, allows researchers to replicate fragments of DNA into the billions of copies needed for analysis, a development that makes *iDNA* analysis fast, accurate, and practical.

That's the good news. The bad news is very bad. According to numbers released by the National Institute of Justice, more than 180,000 rape kits are sitting untested in police evidence lockers around the country. Another 300,000 DNA samples already collected from felons have yet to be analyzed and entered into databases. Worse, 500,000 to one million convicted felons have not had their samples collected despite legislation mandating the procedure.

The total cost of eliminating these backlogs? Less than $2 billion, or half of the more than $4 billion Americans spend on movie tickets each year. Only a handful of states—Virginia, Florida, Texas, New York, and Georgia—have provided the funding necessary to run the system efficiently.

This failure is tragic. As we saw with Isaac Jones, rapists, murderers, and other felons likely to repeat their crimes are being released into our communities while evidence that could potentially link them to other crimes sits unprocessed because of budgetary restraints. In effect, we are measuring a victim's trauma in dollars and cents, letting cases run cold, deceiving victims with assurances that everything is being done to find their assailants. One of the harsh realities of policing is that, without an identified assailant or description to spur investigators, these cases are effectively forgotten.

All the research indicates that victims of sexual assault are tormented by fear and shame years after being attacked. Many are permanently scarred. The evidence also suggests that the knowledge that their attacker has been brought to justice can bring closure.

THE TELL-TALE DNA

Forensics can be defined for our purposes as the use of science and technology to establish facts in criminal investigations and to determine the identity of victims in the aftermath of catastrophic events. *iDNA* typing is already impacting the criminal justice system more dramatically than the introduction of fingerprinting did a hundred years ago, but we've barely scratched the surface of its crime-fighting potential. Long ago, career criminals learned to be careful about leaving fingerprints. *iDNA* extracted from blood, saliva, semen, hair, skin cells, and other biologic traces, is commonplace at crime scenes—tell-tale evidence that until recently could not be harvested. It can be the perspiration a bank robber leaves on a note he passes to a teller; saliva clinging to the back of a postage stamp a kidnapper applies to a ransom note envelope; a droplet of blood spilled by a burglar who cuts himself smashing a window to gain entry to a house; a strand of hair left by a rapist in his victim's bed; skin cells found under the fingernails of the woman who desperately tried to fight him off. *iDNA* analysis assures there are no longer perfect crimes, only imperfect crime-solving procedures.

What you are about to read is not fantasy: New York City prosecutors have indicted the *iDNA* of the Eastside Rapist, a predator who has evaded police dragnets for years. As the statute of limitations drew near, crime lab technicians used semen recovered from his victims to develop an *iDNA* identification of him. It sits in a database against the day a match is found. Without an indictment, the rapist would have been, in effect, absolved of his crimes. In 2003, the city expanded the *iDNA* program to begin indicting hundreds, perhaps thousands of wanted, but as yet unidentified assailants about to escape justice because of the statute of limitations.

Forensic DNA analysis came of age in Leicestershire, England, in 1987. The technology, then time-consuming and inefficient, was deployed to evaluate evidence against a seventeen-year-old male, a kitchen worker in a psychiatric hospital accused of raping and murdering two schoolgirls. Investigators, hoping to build their case, contacted Alec Jeffreys, a University of Leicester geneticist. (The detectives had learned of Jeffreys' success using *iDNA* to link a mother and her child in an immigration proceeding.) In the Leicestershire murder, Jeffreys' tests confirmed the exact opposite: semen retrieved from the victims did not match a blood sample taken from the teenager.

The case unfolded like a Hollywood thriller. The police used expansive investigative powers (and the narrowly focused geographic location of the crime) to demand 4,500 men living in villages adjacent to the crime scene provide blood samples for DNA analysis. The testing took more than a year, but each person cleared narrowed the noose around the killer. The break, which illustrates that community support remains at the heart of successful criminal investigations, came when a bakery manager chatting with employees learned that one of them, Colin Pitchfork, had a colleague donate a blood sample in his stead. The woman reported what she'd heard to the police. Confronted, Pitchfork confessed and his *iDNA* sealed his fate. Joseph Wambaugh retold the story in his best-selling book, *The Blooding*. And Jeffreys, to his surprise, was hailed as the father of forensic DNA.

Word spread quickly. Kevin McElfresh was one of dozens of young scientists fighting to introduce the technology to America. "At the time, I worked for a private lab developing DNA typing for criminal cases," says McElfresh, now general manager at the Bode Technology Group in Springfield, Virginia. "One of the first things we did was start putting together population databases to calculate the probability of finding another human being with the same DNA. Our purpose was to demonstrate that the databases were scientifically reliable. The math was all there. The application was real. Unfortunately, none of us had ever been inside a courtroom. We were a bunch of naive scientists without a clue about who real-life defense attorneys were and how they operated.

"At the time, the only guideline that could help us was *Frye v. United States* (a landmark 1928 case that excluded test results generated by any 'new scientific machine, mechanism, or instrument which is unproven or experimental')," says McElfresh. "So if we could show forensic DNA analysis was generally accepted, we could go forward. It was a great feeling walking into court for the first time and saying, 'This DNA sample matches a known sample of your defendant and the probability of a match like that is one in a trillion.'

"In the past, when prosecutors relied on blood typing to identify suspects, the odds of another person having the same blood type were something like one in forty and one in a hundred. The standard defense response was 'There are six million people in this city. How many individuals does this match?' Then they'd go and slam the victim's character. Now, defense attorneys were faced with their worst nightmare. Not only a positive identification, but having to explain just how it was that semen got into that victim's vagina. The best of them couldn't get around this."

CHAPTER 16

"This Is Going to Be Huge"

In the 1970s, Paul Ferrara, Ph.D., an organic chemist who'd moved south from New York, hopscotching from one unsatisfying corporate job to another, made the leap into crime fighting. By the mid-1980s, Ferrara was director of Virginia's Division of Forensic Science. Unfortunately, he now had to contend with tight budgets, aging equipment, and other frustrations peculiar to forensic science. "It drove me crazy because I always felt forensics while useful, wasn't a very valuable investigative tool," says Ferrara. "We had no way of identifying an individual from any biological or physical material left at a crime scene other than a fingerprint. If the guy put on a pair of gloves, end of story."

BEYOND FINGERPRINTS

In 1986, one of Ferrara's lab directors briefed him on a private sector presentation given at a forensic science convention outlining the new *iDNA* technology. There was a training program for forensic lab technicians. Ferrara was intrigued, but couldn't afford the $60,000 it would cost to train two staff members. "Meanwhile, this is the mid-1980s," he says. "I had any number of molecular biologists and some of my bosses tell me, 'The technology is not far enough along. Let's not get into it.' I was turned down by almost everybody.

"My one ally was Bob Colvin, executive director of the Virginia State Crime Commission. I'd host these office meetings and try to impress my bosses about how revolutionary this stuff was. And they'd say, 'What the hell is DNA?' Fortunately, what I was saying did impress Bob Colvin. He got me in to see A.L. Phillpott, Speaker of Virginia's House of Delegates, a very powerful man, sort of a legend. I made my pitch. Phillpott said, 'I don't know what the hell you're talking about, but I might get you your sixty thousand bucks.' And he did.

"I sent two people for training. It just so happened that in January 1984, a guy began committing a series of very heinous rape/murders in Virginia. His victims were all random—a doctor, a woman who worked for *In Style* magazine, a high-school student. The crimes took place in Arlington, Richmond, and Chesterfield. The killer was dubbed the South Side Strangler.'

"During the investigation, police from various law enforcement jurisdictions disagreed among themselves. All we knew anecdotally was that the killer was leaving lots of seminal fluid. Our lab guys suggested a DNA analysis. We told the law enforcement people we couldn't do it yet, but a private lab could. 'How 'bout we send them the samples so we can at least determine if the murders were done by the same person.' So we did. At that point, a detective with the Arlington County Police Department named Joe Hargas had a suspect. The suspect's name was Timothy Wilson Spencer. Hargas got probable cause to take a blood sample from Spencer. We sent the sample to be processed.

"Sure enough, I get a call saying, 'Paul, it matches Timothy Spencer!' At, that moment, I knew that this was going to be huge. Here's the first capital case in the country and the first serial murder case that had been put together with *iDNA*. In 1994, Spencer became the first person to be executed on the basis of DNA evidence. He never said a word at his trial. Never acknowledged his guilt, but he established that *iDNA* could come through."

There was another twist to the case: an innocent man had already been convicted of murdering Spencer's first victim and he had served five years in prison. He might still be there, if *iDNA* analysis hadn't exonerated him.

PROGRESS CHALLENGED

By the late 1980s, private forensic DNA laboratories working under contract to law enforcement agencies had run up an impressive win streak, providing seemingly incontrovertible identification in scores of cases. Each victory was heralded by a stream of adulatory stories in the media. And then a grisly murder threatened to derail the progress. In February 1987, police arriving at a New York apartment came face-to-face with a tableau of unimaginable horror. Vilma Ponce, seven months pregnant, lay sprawled on the floor, her upper body pierced by more than seventy knife thrusts. Ponce's two-year-old daughter was found butchered in another room. In the course of the investigation, a police officer interviewing Jose Castro, a janitor who worked in a neighboring building, noticed a spot of blood on the man's wristwatch. Castro, linked by other evidence to the crime, was quickly indicted. The bloody wristwatch, along with victims' blood samples was sent for analysis. Lab findings determined the dried blood on Castro's watch was from Vilma Ponce, and the likelihood of another Hispanic having the same genetic fingerprint was one in 829 million.

Castro's defense team, led by Barry Scheck and Peter Neufeld, mounted a challenge to the methodology of the analysis. Their investigation, undertaken by the director of the Massachusetts Institute of Technology's genetics research institute, uncovered discrepancies between prosecution claims and what could accurately be determined from the evidence. The presiding judge ruled the *iDNA* evidence inadmissible. The setback was so devastating that the fact that Castro eventually confessed to the murders was lost in the uproar.

Scheck and Neufeld threatened to undermine the technology at the precise moment it was gaining acceptance. The pair vowed to reopen all convictions won on forensic DNA evidence. At one point, Neufeld even threatened to challenge paternity suits decided by *iDNA*.

An unexpected reversal took place: *iDNA*'s power and enormous potential turned the two defense attorneys into believers. Ultimately, their grievances were about policy and procedure, not the technology. They triggered a hard look at the *iDNA* process, a review of its legal and scientific basis, and ultimately, the implementation of stringent guidelines. Leaders in the field, among them, Richard Roberts, who'd win a Nobel Prize for genetic research, signed a declaration saying the methods used to declare matches and calculate statistics in these cases were unreliable. "It meant prosecutors had to clean up their acts before they ruined *iDNA*'s forensic application," Scheck says.

CHAPTER 17

"I Couldn't Even Spell DNA"

In 1992, a seminal National Academy of Sciences study, "DNA Technology and Forensic Science," set guidelines and professional standards for gathering and processing DNA evidence. New York's Forensic Science Review Board recommended that crime labs win accreditation from the American Society of Crime Laboratory Directors, Laboratory Accreditation Board, a professional licensing body—a standard now adapted across the nation.

A few years later, New York City Police Commissioner Howard Safir was startled to learn there were 12,000 unprocessed rape kits sitting in their medical examiner's office. Without eyewitness identification, with the statute of limitations running, it was possible they'd be discarded.

A stunned Safir headed to Brooklyn where the evidence was gathering dust. "Back then, I couldn't even spell DNA," he recalls. "I didn't have 12,000 rape kits, I had 16,000! The medical examiner told me, 'I can't process them. I don't have enough people or money.' I went to see Rudy [Giuliani] and told him the bad news. He looked at me like I had three heads. I said, 'I need $8 million to contract these kits out to private labs. Then we'll catch rapists!' We realized this was a wonderful issue to push and immediately changed the policy. New York City would analyze every rape kit and compare it with the federal CODIS database." Mayor Giuliani came up with the $8 million, plus an extra $35 million to assure that New York's brand-new crime lab came onboard right.

In 1995, Barry Scheck again leaped into the media spotlight during the O.J. Simpson trial. Brought in by lead attorney Robert Shapiro to advise on the ramifications of *iDNA* evidence (smears of O.J.'s blood were allegedly recovered from Nicole Brown Simpson's body), Scheck conducted a withering, nine-day cross-examination of LAPD forensic scientist Dennis Fung. The verdict hung on the jury's acceptance of the *iDNA* assays. Scheck drove home the possibility that the incriminating evidence had been planted or contaminated by the LAPD, an attack on the process—inadequate handling of the evidence and other procedural issues—rather than the technology. Simpson was found not guilty.

Ironically, *iDNA* technology would become the cornerstone of Scheck and Neufeld's Innocence Project, a legal defense clinic based at the Benjamin N. Cardozo School of Law at Yeshiva University. The project focuses on cases where post-conviction testing of *iDNA* evidence can yield conclusive proof of innocence. "Good forensic science serves everybody," Scheck says today. "It helps apprehend the guilty, but also protects the innocent."

A MASKED STRANGER

On a chilly, gray afternoon in March 1989, terror and violence could not have been further from the mind of Debbie Smith. Secure in a middleclass cocoon in a quiet Southern town, crime to Smith was an inner city phenomenon, something more likely to occur in Richmond or Washington D.C. than in historic Williamsburg, Virginia. It was a typical day for a typical American wife and mother. Smith's two children were at school. Her husband Rob, a lieutenant with the local police department, was asleep in an upstairs bedroom after working a late night shift. Her mind was on the mundane—housekeeping, a dessert she was preparing for dinner, how to spend the thirty dollars in her pocketbook, a birthday present from her mom.

In the laundry room next to the garage, she noticed the clothes dryer was not working properly. Smith unlocked the back door, walked outside to check if the exhaust vent was blocked, something that had happened in the past. She remembered the load of trash that needed to be put out stepped back into the house, leaving the door unlocked. She was headed back out when the stranger came through the backdoor. It took a moment for her to process that a masked stranger stood before her brandishing her son's baseball bat, edging her outside. She broke free, tripped in panic trying to get back into the house. Something hard jabbed into her back. A gun, she thought, as the man whispered he'd kill her. Terrified to call out, she was afraid her cry would send her husband rushing blindly down the stairs where the man waited. "Rob had been up for so long the night before that, even if he heard me, he'd come down thinking I'd cut myself. He would have run right into the guy," she says.

In a wooded area behind the house, he blindfolded her with the T-shirt she was wearing and forced her to the ground. She lay there, tears streaming down her face, the Lord's Prayer on her lips. He raped her, ripping away the sense of security that had defined her life. The man was careful to cover his face, hoping to cloak himself in anonymity, but his *iDNA* clearly marked him. "Remember, I know where you live," the rapist said as he wiped dirt and dead leaves from her jeans. "I'll come back if you tell anyone."

She ran trembling into the house, locked the door, and stumbled up the stairs to her husband. "He got me! Rob, he got me!" In the same moment, threats ringing in her ears, she begged him to ignore what had happened. "All I wanted to do was take a shower," she says. "To wash it all away."

Already feeling the first waves of a monumental tide of guilt, Debbie went with Rob to the hospital. "I got all the questions," she recalls, 'Why didn't you scream? Your husband was right upstairs?' How do I answer that? I felt there was no need for the two of us to die. We have children. If I thought anything while it was happening I thought this part through. I'll always have the 'Why didn't I?' or 'Maybe if I'd done this' haunting me, but I survived, so whatever I did was the right thing."

Unlike so many women who suffer the shame and indignity of assault in silence, Smith made a conscious decision to share her story with others. More than a decade would pass but her resolve would resonate to the Department of Justice and then all the way up to Attorney General John Ashcroft who acknowledged Smith's courage and determination by endorsing legislation to reduce the backlog of unprocessed rape kits.

All of that was far in the future. "The hospital visit proved almost as violating as the actual crime," Smith said later. "I was questioned, probed, plucked, scraped, and swabbed. Everyone was coming at me from all sides—three nurses and a doctor—each wanting something different but always a part of me. I went there defeated because I'd relinquished myself to this stranger. Now these people wanted me to surrender the very clothing off my back."

Smith endured because she believed the evidence contained in her own body would help identify her assailant, and in that way keep other women from becoming victims. "In the beginning, I waited daily to hear the news that they'd found this man," she recalled. As weeks stretched into months and then years, Smith hopes faded even as she realized the rapist would never be gone from her life. She saw him in the worry and concern registered in the eyes of her husband . . . in the rage her son felt because the attacker had brandished *his* baseball bat . . . in her daughter's refusal to leave the porch after dark. And in the unease she observed in her friends and neighbors. "They, too, felt invaded and vulnerable," Smith recalled. "I was a constant reminder that rape can truly happen."

A STRANGER UNMASKED

Over the years, the rapist's power grew. He mocked the alarm systems, the security fence, and the .38 caliber revolver Smith carried in her purse. He smiled when nightmares and obsessions began to erode her sanity, threatening to carry her beyond the reach of loved ones to thoughts of suicide. "Even my faith in God seemed to be failing me," she recalled. "There was no escaping the pain and fear ... I began to realize that I could not and would not live this way. Death seemed to be the only alternative, the answer that would end this horrible nightmare." Ultimately it was her love for her family that prevented Smith from taking her own life, leaving her instead with a kind of death-in-life.

In Richmond, on July 24, 1995, George Li, one of Paul Ferrara's technicians at the Virginia Division of Forensic Science, punched a string of digits into the state database. The numbers were a representation of the *iDNA* of a convicted felon named Norman Jimmerson. Li noted that Jimmerson was already in prison, convicted of kidnapping and robbery charges. He'd attacked two women just weeks before Smith had been assaulted. The software automatically began cross-checking the new data against the stored DNA biometric. The cold hit registered instantaneously. In seconds, it put a name and a face on the man who had haunted Debbie Smith's life for years. Word raced through her husband's police channels jolting Smith like an electric current. "It was one of the most wonderful days," she says.

Unlike the testimony of victims or witnesses, which can be cloudy, confused, or eroded by the relentless attacks of defense attorneys, *iDNA* evidence is incontrovertible. In Smith's case, the wheels of justice suddenly had traction. It took another two years to pierce the smoke-screens thrown up by defense attorneys, but eventually Jimmerson was tried, convicted, and sentenced to two life sentences plus twenty-five years without parole.

"For the first time in years, I could feel myself breathe," Smith told a group of forensic scientists and information specialists gathered at the tenth International Symposium on Human Identification in 1999. "On behalf of myself and many other victims and their families, I want to extend my heartfelt thanks to those of you who work in this field. . . . I didn't realize how powerful DNA is. I don't think everyone realizes how powerful it is." Lost in the applause was the cautionary note Debbie Smith had embedded in her speech: "Anytime a great tool such as DNA is available, yet not used, society commits a crime against its members."

JUSTICE DELAYED IS JUSTICE DENIED

Debbie Smith's words resound in thousands of criminal cases where *iDNA* can balance the scales of justice. One of those is the death sentence handed down to Frank Lee Smith who spent fourteen years on

Florida's death row. An ex-con, Smith was convicted of murdering eight-year-old Shandra Whitehead and sentenced to die in 1985 based on the testimony of a teenage eyewitness.

Convinced of his client's innocence, Smith's attorney worked for four years to come up with another possible suspect, Eddie Lee Mosely, already a suspect in a number of rapes and murders in the Fort Lauderdale area. Armed with an affidavit from the eyewitness retracting her statement, defense attorneys requested that the Florida Supreme Court grant Smith a new trial, and were turned down. Even as *iDNA* testing became more widespread, attempts to have biological evidence from the Whitehead crime scene tested were repeatedly vetoed by the courts.

iDNA eventually linked Eddie Lee Mosely to two other murders, a development that finally convinced authorities to review evidence in the Whitehead case. The results confirmed that Mosely—not Smith—had murdered the child, news that came too late for Smith. Ten months earlier, still moving toward his date with Florida's electric chair, Smith had succumbed to cancer.

CHAPTER 18

Freeing the Innocent, Convicting the Guilty

"We can solve more crimes through DNA testing. It will help us identify missing persons through enhanced DNA methods and techniques. And it will help exonerate individuals who are wrongly convicted of crimes."

ATTORNEY GENERAL JOHN ASHCROFT, MARCH 2003

In a March 2003 press conference, the Department of Justice finally acknowledged the importance of funding *iDNA* technology by announcing an initiative—"Advancing Justice Through DNA Technology"—allocating more than $1 billion over the next five years to improve the use of *iDNA* in the criminal justice system.

Budget shortfalls have slowed the legislation enabling the program, but Washington is now focused on eliminating the backlog of unprocessed rape kits and convicted felon samples that, taken together, total in excess of 480,000 samples. *iDNA*'s ability to identify missing persons, was also trumpeted at the press conference, a step in the inevitable process of using *iDNA* as the gold standard for identity.

COLLECTING *iDNA*

Ideally, in order for this to work, parents will have to decide that a prudent way to reduce risk is to submit their children's samples for profiling which they can store themselves or consign to a secure database. Civilians working in trouble spots around the globe may opt to have an *iDNA* profile databased in the event of tragedy. Here, I want to be clear: to sell, or to turn over the information in these essentially voluntary databases to law enforcement as a screening tool for criminal cases would be an abuse of the technology.

The Department of Defense, through the Armed Forces DNA Identification Laboratory, has already begun to collect the DNA of every man and woman in the armed forces. The samples are not profiled, but stored against the day a need might arise.

The Department of Justice announced it would "not only speed the prosecution of the guilty, but also protect the innocent from wrongful persecution" by funding post-conviction *iDNA* testing for state or federal inmates "who might have been convicted wrongly."

iDNA has been instrumental in the release of at least 127 wrongly convicted individuals. It is logical to assume there are other innocents sitting in prisons while the real perpetrators roam the streets committing new crimes. Frank Lee Smith, the innocent man who died in prison after spending fourteen years on death row, is a reminder that the struggle to win *iDNA* testing in such cases is still ongoing.

CODIS, the federal *iDNA* database, was touted as the principal mechanism for reducing the testing backlog. Paul Ferrara, Howard Safir, and others who have worked with CODIS complain the system is using outdated technology. The government promised expanded testing capability, training, technology upgrades, and research. According to the Department of Justice, there are more than 130 public crime labs capable of conducting DNA testing, but fewer than 10 percent have the automated facilities needed to conduct efficient testing. This very problem has led states such as New York and Virginia to outsource their DNA tests to private labs.

"DNA technology is becoming widely used in so many applications, the public labs cannot possibly keep up," says Paul Ferrara. "A rape or murder case can consist of hundreds of pieces of evidence, which must be tested for the presence of biological materials. Investigators and prosecutors keep asking 'Where's the DNA evidence?' If it's not examined, the defense attorney is going to ask why. There is no way to get around a laborious, careful scrutiny of all the evidence. To do that in a timely fashion requires more resources. That's why the public laboratories depend on the private labs. If it weren't for the private guys we'd be in worse shape."

If one looks past looming budgetary shortfalls and the political minefield to be crossed before the proposals becomes law, we get a clear idea at where the technology is headed. Every state and the federal government require that *iDNA*, like fingerprints and mug shots, be taken from certain convicted criminals. However, the states differ in how aggressively samples are collected. Some limit their *iDNA* collection to sex offenders; others have shied away from including individuals who have committed lesser felonies like burglary. Twenty-three states require that DNA identification samples be collected from all convicted criminals.

Virginia has been collecting DNA from all felons since 1990; its DNA database contains more than 200,000 profiles. By the fall of 2003, the state had solved 99 homicides and nearly 200 sexual assaults, numbers that continue to grow. Florida has been similarly aggressive. Cecelia Crouse, director of the Palm Beach County sheriff's forensic DNA lab reports that *iDNA* analysis, in conjunction with other investigative tools and leads, now helps solve 250 crimes a year.

In Virginia, 82 percent of the matches would not have occurred if that state's *iDNA* database had been limited to violent offenders. In Florida, 45 percent of the state's cold hits on homicide and rape cases came from *iDNA* taken from individuals who'd been convicted of burglary. As the Department of Justice puts it, "What had once seemed reasonable: that you only needed to collect and inventory *iDNA* samples from those who had been convicted of assault, doesn't seem to be borne out in fact. Collecting samples from the broad spectrum of criminals will help us solve crimes which appear to be unrelated."

Paul Ferrara, who pioneered the convicted felon DNA database, has taken the program to another level. In January 2003, Virginia began recording the *iDNA* of all suspects charged with "recordable arrests," i.e., crimes in which the law mandates fingerprints be taken.

"We're in the middle of a revolution," agrees Howard Safir. "Almost every day, new DNA laws are passed, most of them expanding the collection process. My position is that we ought to take DNA at the point of arrest. Everyone who is arrested in England has his or her DNA taken, using a 'Buccal swab,' that takes DNA samples from inside the subject's cheek. The sample is sent off to the Forensic Science Service for analysis and database comparison."

Safir likes to tell the story of the turn-of-the-century police commissioner, "who heard about this great new technology in England called fingerprinting. At the time the NYPD was identifying people using something called the Bertillon System which used cameras to measure the distance between your right ear and your eye, the length of one foot and stuff like that. It was crazy. In 1904, the commissioner sent a Sergeant Murphy to England to learn fingerprinting. Six months later, the NYPD solved its first homicide using fingerprints. The English are ahead of us again. Since 1995, law enforcement in the United Kingdom has helped provide information on more than 100,000 crimes using *iDNA*."

THE ROAD AHEAD

Like link analytics, *iDNA* is a disruptive technology. In a relatively short period of time, it has challenged the very basis for identification, displacing less accurate and fallible systems. In doing so, it has delivered on part of its great promise: helping free the innocent and bring justice to the guilty, identifying the remains of soldiers and disaster victims who would otherwise go unknown. Much more needs to be done. Real progress in bringing *iDNA* technology to the next level— societal acceptance, legislative safeguards, adequate funding, broad implementation—requires that legitimate questions and pressing concerns over policy be put to rest.

It is possible that answers to the eternal questions—who lives to a ripe old age, who dies young, who triumphs, who falters, who becomes a saint or a sinner—are contained within the twin strands of DNA's helix. Such questions have intrigued scientists and theologians for centuries. However, as we've seen, they cannot be studied, analyzed, or answered using *iDNA*.

There are real issues beginning to surface and we must confront them head-on to prevent the misuse of DNA technology.

- We should not create databases containing the *iDNA* of individuals cleared of or never charged with crimes.

- We must guard against the potential for DNA dragnets where investigators collect DNA samples without a person's written consent from large numbers of individuals in order to eliminate suspects.

- At no time should a person provide his or her DNA for one purpose—to solve a specific crime, for example—and the sample later be stored in a databank or used for another purpose without their informed consent.

- We need to address the issues surrounding *iDNA* matches that do not hit on all thirteen identity markers extracted from evidence. If the system determines nine or ten loci matches, you may get varying numbers of "potential suspects," all but one who are obviously innocent, yet who may come under the cloud of criminal investigation.

- *iDNA* should be used as part of a "complete" case, along with any other information recovered or developed at a crime scene (from the make and model of the getaway car to a suspect's hair color). With genetic information, it's critical that partial DNA information not be prejudicial to the triers of fact and the jury. It must be presented in a proper manner.

- *iDNA* samples used to create databases of convicted felons should only be used for forensic identification and to make sure lab work is right in terms of quality assurance. Nothing else. This includes so called "convenience samples"—the DNA of convicted rapists, pedophiles, and people who have a proclivity toward violence—that researchers may find valuable when studying criminal behaviors. However, this is an improper use of forensic identification technology.

• As soon as an identity is confirmed, we can destroy the *iDNA* collected for purposes as a "reference" sample. We can always obtain another sample in the future if need be.

As we've seen, the standards society uses to establish identity are both fragile and vulnerable. This fundamental weakness lies behind much of the risk we face today. *iDNA's* ability to anchor identity can blunt that assault. In the near future, identity, so weakened by fallible representations like birth dates and Social Security numbers, will be anchored by infallible genetic markers. *iDNA's* significance as a crime-solving technology will be complemented by its importance in safe-guarding identity. A database containing the *iDNA* of police, firemen, and rescue workers would have prevented the additional pain endured in the aftermath of September 11th when victims' family members were forced to bring in toothbrushes and strands of hair hoping to find cells that could identify their loved ones.

Scientists and the victims will continue to help move society closer to the day when *iDNA* is commonplace. Debbie Smith was among those present at a government's press conference in March 2003. Like many, she was of two minds, excited and frustrated. Too much time had passed, she said, since Rep. Carolyn Maloney (D-NY) introduced legislation in 2002 to help reduce the backlog of untested rape evidence kits. Various pieces of legislation were reconfigured and reintroduced in 2003. At the beginning of 2004, the law had cleared the Senate and was awaiting action in the House. "I have a really hard time with all the hurry up and wait," Smith says. "It just needs to get done."

PART V

GUIDELINES FOR USING TECHNOLOGY RESPONSIBLY

Throughout, I've stressed that technology is value neutral. Right and wrong, good and evil are judgments best reserved for how man chooses to deploy technology. As an elementary school student in Sayville, I discovered "Our Friend the Atom" at the same time I was taking cover in the air-raid drills of the early 1960s. Information technology is as powerful and disruptive a technology as nuclear fission. It must be handled with respect. Used responsibly, it has enormous potential for good. Knowledge can shelter us from the threats that shadow our lives and the well being of our nation.

Over time, I believe a fair and open information exchange can help defuse much of the animosity and misunderstanding bubbling across the world. The irresponsible use of information-privacy invasion, surveillance, redlining, or blacklisting—runs counter to the very democratic principles we are trying to defend and preserve.

The chapters that follow apply a "decision rules" construct to some of the high risk situations we're likely to encounter in the days ahead—in effect, a blueprint for determining the responsible use of information. Obviously, provisions for protecting and guaranteeing privacy are central to this construct. When the benefits of deploying information technology do not offset the risks it may create, privacy protection should prevail. Embedded in these pages is a call for an honest dialogue based on facts and passionate beliefs, rather than generic, emotion-fueled hypothetical scenarios. Certainly, it's long overdue and must include interested, concerned, and impacted parties on all sides of the information technology debate.

CHAPTER 19

What We Need Are Decision Rules

In the winter of 2002, the Pentagon announced a plan to develop a "virtual, centralized grand database" containing information on the routine activities of millions of Americans as a weapon in the war on terrorism. The data, encompassing phone and travel records, driver's license applications, credit card and other financial transactions, even images captured by surveillance cameras, would be combined with intelligence and other information into what the Department of Defense called the "Total Information Awareness" or TIA system. Data-mining algorithms would scour this massive repository for behavior, patterns, or associations that might suggest a terrorist conspiracy.

The project, under the auspices of the Defense Advanced Research Project Agency (DARPA), the agency that contributed the financial support and technical wherewithal to jumpstart the Internet, was designed to counter the asymmetric threat posed by terrorist groups.

The plan was immediately attacked by civil liberties groups as well as Democratic and Republican, liberal and conservative politicians.

In the spring of 2003, the U.S. Senate, reacting to fears over the "surveillance society" TIA seemed to herald, voted to halt funding of the technology—since renamed the Terrorism Information Awareness project—until its potential for abuse had been examined. By the fall of 2003, retired Admiral John Poindexter who'd spearheaded TIA, had been forced to resign, and the program was cancelled.

Total Information Awareness sparked such outrage because it violated standards of both privacy *and* logic. If you're looking for the needle in the haystack—the infinitesimal percentage of the population that might be engaged in a terrorist or criminal conspiracy—piling on more hay compounds the difficulty. To the average person reading a newspaper or hearing about the plan on the radio during the morning commute, the idea of the government snooping through enormous amounts of personal information seemed more threatening than the risk it was designed to counter.

The failure to formulate consistent, logical standards governing the use of information triggers much of the controversy swirling around these technologies. In this chapter, I introduce the concept of "decision rules," a blueprint to guide our thinking when making information/risk mitigation decisions. These are not hard and fast rules—society must implement those—but approaches to rationalizing the decision-making process.

Decision rules apply to identifiable threats—risks many of us are likely to encounter in our daily lives—not vague scenarios or future possibilities. They are specific, but far-reaching. Applied consistently, they will mitigate today's threat, but also identify standards of prudent behavior that will reduce risk over time. Some may be codified as law and regulation; others are simply guidelines for making informed choices.

Decision rules are grounded in the idea that the exchange of information must be consensual. (Obviously, there are exceptions: ongoing criminal investigations, specific national security concerns, etc.) Practically speaking, this is already the case. We consent to share information when we apply for jobs, credit, and many kinds of benefits and privileges. (For example, applying for a driver's license when we relocate to a new state automatically triggers scrutiny of our past driving history.) Decision rules govern how our information may (or may not) be used in less familiar, or more complex risk-management situations.

MAKING RULES

The key to that vital question—how do we tap information effectively, legitimately, and judiciously?—lies in the construct that follows. I've also provided examples that illustrate the appropriate application of (or failure to apply) logical standards. In the latter case, risk actually may increase, as will the potential for other negative consequences such as privacy violations.

Decision Rule 1: *Identify the specific risk*. Information technology must be marshaled against specific threats both real and ongoing. Risk must be clearly described before it can be mitigated. In effect, it must be isolated from the background clutter of vague, emotional, or potential concerns. Clearly, the enormous, amorphous net cast by the Total Information Awareness program violated this first standard of specific rather than generic risk assessment and understanding.

Decision Rule 2: *Determine what information exists or could be made available to mitigate the specific risk we're attempting to address*. In 2004, for example, more than 23 million foreign nationals will enter the United States on visas. (Millions more will come from Europe and other "visa-waiver" countries like Japan and Australia.) Clearly, our government has an interest in vetting these visitors—a percentage of whom represents real threat—before they cross our borders. Such threat information, including validation of their true identity is often documented in their home countries. Yet, this has never been routinely exchanged between governments despite its obvious relevance to worldwide risk reduction. Valuable reference information could also be collected at the point of entry, providing identity and reference information for future trips into the country.

Decision Rule 3: *Determine the legitimacy of the available information.* What available information (or information that might be made available) does society deem legitimate and appropriate to mitigate the specific risk being addressed? Appropriate information must demonstrate clear, consistent, and verifiable evidence of risk reduction. Not all data meeting these criteria is appropriate. Some information may create secondary risk. Or risk may be reduced, but not significantly enough to warrant use. Over time, multiple applications of data (so-called "mission creep") may create cumulative risk, a chilling effect that must be monitored and if need be, addressed. History tells us the heavy-handed use of information—the internal passports favored by police states—will choke off the very democracy we're trying to protect. Here again, the Total Information Awareness program's intent to create a "virtual, grand centralized database" fails because no clear association between the data to be tapped and the specific risk to be mitigated had been established.

Decision Rule 4: *Determine who is allowed access and who sets the decision criteria.* Responsibility for accessing legitimate, accurate, complete, and timely data rests with the individual or entity accountable for the consequences should risk become reality. In short, those society deems have a "need to know." This responsibility can be limited in scope (parent, landlord, merchant, day-care operator), or extend all the way up to the federal government. Often, it's overlapping; responsibility may shift as accountability increases. In some cases, access and the right to set standards may lie with different entities. For example, airlines have access to watch-list data, but the Transportation Security Administration sets the rules the air carriers must follow in using the information to screen passengers.

Decision Point 1: At this point in our construct, a decision must be made: do I make a decision using the available, legitimized information to mitigate a known, specific risk? Or, do I make a decision irrespective of the available date? Assuming I choose to use the legitimized information, I must move to the next step in the decision rule.

Decision Rule 5: *Create mechanisms to adjudicate instances where the correlation between information and addressable risk is unclear.* Sometimes, we reach the limits of technology: no clear red or green signal can be ascertained from available information. Generally, this is where things can go awry. Adjudication is a critical component of the decision rule construct. Technology is marching us into an era of automated decision making, which, by its very nature, is not precise. It's vital, to our definition of the responsible use of information, that a sophisticated, nuanced adjudication process—governed by humans rather than machines—be in place. In a risky world, yellow is just as significant as red unless the uncertainty can be removed and the caution light changed to green.

Decision Point 2: At this point, based upon the results of adjudication, a second decision is made that resolves uncertain or unclear ("yellow") situations. The rational for the decision made is clear and easily explained, and, where necessary and appropriate, subject to the due process of an appeal or decision review.

Decision Rule 6: *Ensure the information/risk mitigation construct is dynamic.* Standards will continue to emerge or require amendment. Often risk escalates; sometimes it goes away. It's never static. Over time, risk reduction and a particular data set may no longer correlate; access to this information is now inappropriate. New information may become available; it should be evaluated and used if deemed legitimate.

TWO SPECIFIC OUTCOMES

The decision rule process hs two specific outcomes:

Decision Result 1: *Significant positive or negative consequences* will flow from how (or whether) these rules are applied in real-world risk situations.

Decision Result 2: *Standards of prudent behavior* will emerge as a result of the positive or negative consequences.

A final point: the positive consequences that consistently flow from the appropriate, responsible use of information will be self-reinforcing, creating what might be called "a virtuous cycle," where prudent behavior is reinforced by positive results, making the entire system stronger.

Today there are no clearly accepted policies describing or enabling the responsible use of information. There are policies, but there is still not consensus or broad acceptance of the concept of information's value for good. In my view, this failing lies at the heart of the privacy debate. Ignoring the need for a rational, far-reaching information policy opens the door to conflict and catastrophe. As the examples that follow make clear, decision rules work. Whether or not we employ them as a framework for responsible decision making in an increasing risky world is our choice.

CHAPTER 20

Rules in the Real World

Let's apply decision rules to a series of real world situations. Our first example asks the question, should day-care center workers be subjected to background checks? Based on the evidence, it would seem appropriate to screen day-care center employees before allowing them access to our children. However, absent enforceable local, state, or national standards, each day-care operator must decide whether or not to pay for and utilize available legitimate information to counter the risk of a potential or current employee knowingly posing a risk to children. In this circumstance, at least four decision rules can be applied:

• **Decision Rule 1:** *Identify the risk*. Obviously, the fact that predators are drawn to institutions and organizations that provide them with access to children constitutes a very real risk.

• **Decision Rules 2 & 3:** *Determine what legitimate information exists to reduce the risk.* Public information contained in criminal records and online sex offender registries can identify those who should not be allowed access to children. The data has also been deemed legitimate and appropriate for use in screening day-care workers.

• **Decision Rule 4:** *Determine who is allowed access and who sets decision criteria.* The person accountable for the risk—the day-care operator—has the right to access the information and use it for the permissible purposes established by law or regulation.

Here, our day-care operator reaches Decision Point 1, to screen or not. If the person does not act (and society or parents do not intervene) to screen employees, and the preventable risk of a child being harmed becomes reality, society will (and must) hold the day-care center accountable.

It's important to note that risk can never be reduced to zero. If that same day-care center operator does screen employees using appropriate, available information tools, and the worst happens despite her best efforts, she can argue that they followed prudent standards of behavior and should not be found negligent.

TERRORISM AND WATCH LISTS

The link between an individual on a federal watch list and terrorism is significant and real. As we know, government agencies were aware before September 11th that the hijackers Khalid Al-Midhar and Nawaf Alhazmi had attended an Al-Qaeda summit in Malaysia before arriving in the United States. (Rememeber the CIA had tracked the pair's arrival in California before backing off its surveillance.) A standard of prudent behavior flows from this particular piece of information: Passengers should not be allowed to board an airplane without being screened against watch lists. (Note that this construct does not support profiling or statistical inference as an effective way to identify terrorists.)

Airline security personnel should have had access to watch-list information and applied that information in screening passengers. (Both hijackers bought plane tickets using their real names.) However, in the real world, other interests and concerns often obscure the obvious: airline schedules must be met; politics or financial gain, not terrorism, has historically driven hijacking; increased security equals increased costs; confidentiality of passenger information must be maintained, etc.

In this circumstance, the following decision rules and standards were applicable:

• **Decision Rule 1:** *Identify the risk.* A known terrorist seeking to board a commercial airliner constitutes a clear and present danger.

• **Decision Rule 2 & 3:** *Determine what legitimate information exists to reduce the risk.* Al-Midhar and Alhazmi were both on a federal terrorist watch list. Reviewing watch lists is a required part of the granting a person the right to fly.

• **Decision Rule 4:** *Determine who is allowed access and who sets decision criteria.* Watch list information should have been accessed by airline security personnel who, in turn, should have enforced federal rules preventing such individuals from getting anywhere near an airplane.

• **Decision Point 1:** Sometime prior to September 11th, we must assume that we were not sufficiently motivated, or simply failed, to effectively share terrorist watch-list information with the airlines. The technology was available. The information correlated. The risk was sufficiently elevated to justify deploying the data. The two men were known to be in the United States. Yet, Al-Midhar and Alhazmi were not detained when they boarded American Airlines Flight 77, which they hijacked and crashed into the Pentagon, a negative consequence all the more terrible because of the logic that predicted it and the tools available to prevent it.

One of the outcomes of our decision rule construct predicts that *standards of prudent behavior will emerge*. Today, watch-list information is being shared, but still not as smoothly or consistently as one would hope. On September 11th, 2001, the failure to apply these logical decision rules led to the ultimate negative consequence, one of the most horrific loses of life in our nation's history.

RISK ON THE ROAD

Every day, thousands of trucks containing toxic chemicals, fuel oil, munitions, and medical waste make their way across the country. Anyone driving one of these rigs can inflict catastrophic damage on society. There is appropriate information—driving histories, DUI records, etc.—available to mitigate this significant risk by screening drivers. (As for concerns about drivers being part of a terrorist conspiracy and criminal enterprise, link analytics can delve for nonobvious connections between drivers and known terrorists or criminals.) Operators of freight carriers should have "need to know" access to the data. Based on that information, they decide whether or not to hire potential employees. Here, as with day care or terrorism, the responsibility for developing and enforcing a standard may shift to government agencies as part of their duty to protect society.

One side note: Our government continues to struggle with how to implement a new hazardous material program. Under the USA PATRIOT Act, the Transportation Security Administration (TSA) is required to do a security threat assessment of all holders of commercial driver's licenses who currently have, or apply for, a Hazardous Materials Endorsement (HME). In 2003, the TSA published an Interim Final Rule and an amended Interim Final Rule, neither of which provided standards for obtaining fingerprints, biographical information, or criminal history information. The result is that currently no, or at best limited, security threat assessments are under away with respect to HMEs. Even when this is finally enforced (the deadline now is December 1, 2004, which many believe is an aggressive deadline), trucking companies will not get direct access to relevant criminal history information. Instead, the TSA, working with state driver's license agencies, will green light the issuance or the renewal of an HME or will decline to do so.

Why the delays? One answer: unlike September 11th, this kind of mass casualty catastrophe—imagine a trailer full of fuel oil or toxic chemicals exploding in New York City's Holland Tunnel—hasn't happened. Good news, but a terrible standard for threat assessment. To most of us, background screening doesn't violate a driver's civil rights or impose undue financial burdens on the trucking company. However, the driver or the trucking company employing him or her might argue otherwise, sometimes with merit, that a solid employment history is evidence enough to waive more intense, on-going scrutiny. Screening, they argue, results in increased operating costs that may create a competitive disadvantage, especially for a smaller company.

Logic dictates a company should screen its drivers. However, that company may decide the risk it faces is minuscule, mitigated by insurance coverage and other factors. According to our construct, the obligation of state or federal authorities to protect the citizenry from a chemically impaired or rogue driver and the considerable damage that might occur trumps all other arguments.

Here the following decision rules and standards are applicable:

• **Decision Rule 1:** *Identify the risk.* Clearly the driver of one of these rigs may knowingly or accidentally inflict catastrophic damage.

• **Decision Rule 2 & 3:** *Determine what legitimate information exists to reduce the risk.* Information technology provides real-time access to operators' driving records, histories of DUIs, criminal records, etc. Employment screening is a permissible purpose for using this information.

• **Decision Rule 4:** *Determine who is allowed access and who sets decision criteria.* The trucking companies—the parties responsible for the risk—must (and do) have access to the information. Today, the decision to use the information is discretionary. However, the government is exercising its duty to mitigate catastrophic risk by setting the decision criteria in the form of mandatory driver screening in the future.

• **Decision Rule 5:** *Create an adjudication mechanism when there is uncertainty.* There will be times when the decision to hire a potential driver is unclear because the accuracy or interpretation of the information may be in doubt. An effective process of a human review of the data must be in place to quickly and fairly resolve the uncertainty. Here, a doctrine of transparency and empathy should prevail.

VETTING AIRPORT SCREENERS

In the spring of 2002, the Transportation Security Administration ordered background checks on more than 112,000 candidates who had applied for airport screening positions—the men and women who scrutinize us and our baggage before we board an airplane. The process involved extensive and thorough investigation of credit, criminal record, employment and educational histories, along with verifiable personal references. A color-coded scheme—green, yellow, red—was used to classify each candidate's qualifications based on the results of the background checks and other established criteria. In the real world, men and women don't always fit neatly into categories. Of the 112,000 candidates screened, nearly half, were originally classified as yellow or "decisional." Candidates classified "yellow" were given additional consideration and scrutiny by the TSA or its contractors, until a fair and conclusive decision could be made in each and every case. Here, the number of people requiring adjudication of uncertainty was abnormally high, due primarily to the government's decision criteria which demonstrated an understanding of the negative consequences of hiring someone with a disqualifying characteristic, but also of not hiring someone who was legitimately qualified. In vetting TSA screeners, the following decision rules and standards were applied:

• **Decision Rule 1:** *Identify the risk.* The possibility of a member of a terrorist "sleeper" cell assuming responsibility for assuring airline security constitutes an enormous risk. To a lesser degree, so do known criminals and sociopaths.

• **Decision Rule 2 & 3:** *Determine what legitimate information exists to reduce the risk.* Extensive information—credit histories, criminal records, employment and educational histories, personal references, links to known terrorists or criminal associates—were all available.

• **Decision Rule 4:** *Determine who is allowed access and who sets decision criteria.* The Transportation Security Administration, the federal agency ultimately charged with reducing the risk of air travel, is granted access and also sets the decision criteria.

• **Decision Rule 5:** *Create an adjudication mechanism when there is uncertainty.* A comprehensive human adjudication process was in place and provided both a resolution process for all "decisional" or yellow candidates and an appeal mechanism to ensure due process to candidates that failed the decision criteria.

RELEARNING THE LESSONS OF HISTORY

History tells us the failure to apply logic to decision making often has tragic consequences. Here's one of the most troubling examples: On February 19, 1942, just two months after Pearl Harbor, President Franklin Delano Roosevelt signed Executive Order 9066 mandating the evacuation of more than 120,000 Americans of Japanese heritage into internment camps. Over the next three years, loyal Americans who were deemed national security risks simply because of their ethnicity were uprooted—forced to leave home, schools, and businesses—to live in squalid conditions in camps scattered across the Western states. We now know the risk they allegedly represented was nonspecific, and in fact, nonexistent. No legitimate information existed to substantiate or eliminate this supposed threat. There were no adjudication mechanisms; no decision criteria save ethnicity. (When profiling is used as a standard, all too often everyone fitting the profile is considered a threat. The tendency is to expand the population of people identified as potential threats, instead of creating a very narrow set of people who represent a real risk.) Emotion, the bane of logic, was running high in the aftermath of Pearl Harbor—so high that the U.S. Supreme Court upheld the process in 1943 and again in 1944. The result: one of the more shameful and irrational episodes in American history. Forty years would pass before Congress awarded formal compensation to surviving internees, but the shame and suffering endured by these loyal Americans can never be erased.

Were lessons learned? In many cases, no, because no broadly accepted decision rule process has been adopted. Between 1988 and 1991, for example, vehicles driven by African-Americans along a particular stretch of the New Jersey Turnpike accounted for 13.5 percent of the total traffic and approximately 15 percent of the speeders. Yet that 13.5 percent accounted for 46 percent of all vehicles stopped by police. What set of decision rules (other than racial profiling) could possibly have yielded this kind of disproportionate result?

The same was true in 1992 when police videotapes indicated that African-Americans accounted for approximately 10 percent of the motorists driving along a Florida stretch of I-95, yet they comprised 70 percent of those pulled over. There was a similar scenario along I-95 in parts of Maryland. There was no specific identifiable risk, no legitimate information—certainly race alone cannot be a primary factor to justify pulling over one particular motorist over any other. No review process of the decision criteria, no reasonable adjudication. In short, no application of logical and fair standards. This type profiling is wrong, even antithetical to democracy. Had decision rules, not human emotions, been used, perhaps these types of situations could have been avoided.

We continue to struggle precisely because there is no widely accepted framework for making information-based decisions. All too often emotion carries the day, and standards of prudent behavior are very slow to emerge. For example, fewer than half the states in America have laws requiring all motorcyclists to wear helmets. (Some have actually repealed such statutes.) Yet, when we identify the risk, it turns out that the fatality rate for motorcyclists involved in accidents is 3.6 times higher than that of individuals involved in car wrecks. Legitimate information is available to mitigate such risk: research indicates motorcyclists wearing helmets are much less likely to suffer head trauma in crashes. The cost of treating such trauma is 80 percent higher than that of individuals injured wearing helmets. The fact that motorists in collisions with motorcyclists are at fault 70 percent of the time is meaningless information, particularly if I'm paralyzed in an intensive care ward.

Health-care providers, legislators, advocacy groups, and the motorcycle-riding public have access to the data. Yet, the right to ride unfettered has become a hot button emotional issue, a mad crusade fueled by myth, a type of bad information. Libertarians insist individuals have the right to convert themselves into road kill, a logic as egregious as the arguments that helmets cause neck and spinal cord injuries. The biggest myth may be that motorcyclists are independent pioneers exercising that archetypal American prerogative of being left alone. That fallacy was exposed by the U.S. Supreme Court in *Simon v. Governor of the Commonwealth of Massachusetts*: "From the moment of the injury, society picks the person up off the highway; delivers him to a municipal hospital and municipal doctors; provides him with unemployment compensation; if, after recovery, he cannot replace his lost job, and if the injury causes permanent disability, may assume the responsibility for his and his family's continued subsistence. We do not understand the state of mind that permits plaintiff to think that only he himself is concerned."

States still have conflicting helmet laws because risk, emotion, and bad information have not been offset by available and legitimate "good data." At the moment, this is what society has decided. And it is for society to choose. Yet, our construct tells us that over time, if the risk is compelling enough, standards of prudent behavior will emerge and create a societal tipping point. The question is how many years, how many deaths, and shattered lives will it take?

CHAPTER 21

A National Discussion on Privacy

The decision rule framework allows society to determine the appropriate use of information technology. At the same time, decision rules safeguard privacy, a delicate balancing act that must take into account the power of information, democratic principles, and the high-risk environment in which we find ourselves. This challenge may be framed as a debate between those of us supporting the responsible use of information technology and those seeking to limit or prevent its application—an exchange that should be governed by common sense, common decency, compromise, and the ultimate realization that we share common ground.

Unfortunately, this has not been the case. Arguments on both sides of the "privacy debate" have been shrill, emotional, fueled by scare tactics, and grounded in vague threats and generic concerns. The Total Information Awareness scheme described in an earlier chapter is a perfect example. As are the fears of privacy invasion raised in an attempt to short-circuit an Arizona school board's 2004 plan to install video cameras and facial recognition software to keep wanted criminals and known predators away from students.

What should be a vibrant and vital debate has been marginalized by what Dr. Alan F. Weston calls "privacy fundamentalists" who, heedless of risk and regardless of safeguards, don't want personal information circulated or shared under any circumstances, and the "privacy unconcerned," individuals who don't care or are willing to overlook privacy incursions. In total, these individuals and groups account for more than 40 percent of the American public. The rest of us, Westin says, are "privacy pragmatists." We want to know what data we're being asked to share, how sensitive it is, to what purpose, and under what protections. We want a balance between privacy *and* risk reduction. Based on that calculus, we decide whether a particular program or application is good or bad. We decide, because the vast majority of information applications are and should remain consensual when accessing information or when seeking a privilege.

The imbalance is reflected in the bewildering patchwork of federal and state privacy statutes. (State legislators introduce more than 5,000 such bills each year.) Many of these laws are incomplete, overlapping, and occasionally contradictory. Most are concerned with regulating or limiting where information comes from, rather than content, sensitivity, or usage—the issues Americans really care about.

Technology complicates matters further, rocketing data across state lines and jurisdictions in nanoseconds. What could be harder for the private citizen, government, or legitimate business user of information to figure out than which laws apply in a given situation? Is it the law in the state where the data source resides? The law where the consumer lives? Statutes regulating the end user?

The onrush of technology will continue, creating as Mike Kami predicts, ever-escalating levels of stress, and potentially greater privacy concerns. In the year 2020, surveillance cameras and automobile tracking systems like EZ Pass and Fas Trac will have proliferated. Telltale radio frequency identification devices (RFIDs) will be embedded in consumer products, potentially in the clothes we wear. Cell phones/cameras and wireless devices will have GPS capabilities pinpointing our location at all times. For example, a number of telecom companies have announced that in 2004, they will begin offering so-called "backpack trackers," small GPS devices that can be placed, for example, in a child's backpack. A parent can go to a password-protected website, enter the unique identification number of the tracker hidden away in their child's backpack; and, in real-time, locate the tracker within fifty feet.

Several phone companies are about to offer a consensual service allowing an individual to pull up on his cell phone screen an indication of whether a list of preselected cell phone numbers (i.e., people) is in the same vicinity. A businessperson traveling from Washington, D.C. to the West Coast can determine upon arriving at LAX whether any of as many as several hundred friends, family members, or colleagues are in the area. It seems to me that location and tracking information is every bit as sensitive as medical and financial information and should be subject to decision rules.

These are developments—many of them positive for many applications—that must be examined rationally rather than emotionally. As we stand on the edge of this uncharted world, it seems to me that we have three choices. The first is to "Let 'er rip," basically to unleash technology, blind and unchecked, on society. This argument gleefully proclaims "the genie is out of the bottle—deal with it." This position is as wrong as it is dangerous. A second choice, equally troublesome, is to legislate and litigate the march of information to a standstill. Here, personal anonymity—not privacy—is elevated to a constitutional right, an absolute where information's protective power is bled away, even as our enemies continue to turn technology against us. The third choice—in my view, our only real option—is to strive for both privacy and security by building rational constructs and national consensus on the responsible use of information.

At a less risky moment in history, legislators and legal scholars could parse, nuance, and refine privacy endlessly, until some balance is struck between privileged personal information and, "need to know," between *ideal* and *real*. We don't live in a vacuum. Nor do we live in the comforts of an academic environment.

Grinding bureaucracies spewing out simplistic laws intended to shut down the information flow at the source are ineffective at best, wildly dangerous at worst. The consequences play out every day. In the winter of 2003, Charles Cullen, a licensed critical-care nurse, was charged with the murder of a patient under his care at the Somerset Medical Center in Somerville, New Jersey. Under questioning, Cullen, whose career spanned sixteen years and ten different hospitals in Jersey and Pennsylvania, told investigators that he'd murdered between thirty and forty patients over the years by administering lethal overdoses of pharmaceuticals to alleviate their "pain and suffering."

It turned out that early in his career, Cullen had been investigated after patients in his care died unexpectedly. He'd also been a suspect in a series of drug thefts and other infractions. What seems most shocking is that he'd been fired from at least *four of his last seven jobs*. Yet, privacy safeguards in the form of confidentiality rules (and the fear of lawsuits such rules engender among employers) kept Somerset Medical Center administrators from learning anything of Cullen's past. Somerset president and CEO Dennis Miller told reporters for the *Philadelphia Inquirer* that since Cullen had never been convicted of a crime or disciplined in New Jersey or Pennsylvania, his record was clean. One after another, former employers admitted they'd provided Somerset nothing beyond dates of Cullen's employment. Here's privacy and legal liability twisted beyond recognition.

By January 2004, police in seven different jurisdictions were reportedly investigating murder allegations against Cullen. Prosecutors were flooded with calls from distraught families forced to confront the horror that a loved one might have died under the malignant caregiver, a person upon whom society bestows trust and responsibility. "If you have not been convicted of a crime, as this guy had not—he'd been investigated— that falls below the radar screen," Dennis Miller told the *Inquirer*. "We did everything right, and now we have to change the way things are done."

Somewhere, information that might have prevented this outrage was locked away. It was private, privileged, excluded from both caregivers and patients. Is privacy the right to leave a trail of mounting evidence and suspicion that cannot even be whispered because of standards that make a mockery of other human beings' rights to safety and security? Can we not put in place a process that respects the right of the individual to be free of harmful rumor and innuendo, yet provides society with the protections it needs from those with ill and evil intent?

What do Americans want in terms of privacy? The research suggests that privacy is personal—no two people define privacy the same way. We care about the abuse of our Social Security numbers because we all have them. We care about privacy invasions across the Internet because nearly 90 percent of the American public has access to cyberspace. We care less, for instance, about access and availability of criminal records. Certainly, we'd want to know that our health-care provider has been suspected of murder. It's our medical records we want protected. To paraphrase author David Brin, we want privacy for ourselves, but accountability for everyone else.

Privacy has been marginalized. It must be returned to the mainstream. Privacy concerns have been generalized, emotionalized. We must address them specifically and rationally: how do we use information to make our airports, schools and day-care centers safe, our financial transactions and employment practices secure, while respecting individual rights? How do we keep our approaches—as decision rules demand—logical, flexible, and dynamic as risk waxes and wanes?

We can begin by agreeing to some simple ground rules:

- The discussion should be based on a real risk, not a hypothetical or "what if" scenario.

- The debate should be passionate, but not emotional. Baseless claims only make for bad policy. We need to stick to the facts, but defend our positions with vigor.

- We should debate the use of information, not the availability. Information exists, and it can be used for good and bad. The way to ensure it is used for the good of society is to set strict rules for when information can be used, by whom, and for what purpose. Strict penalties for violating the rules should also come into play. Today, we have few, if any, of either.

- We must keep in mind that the *sensitivity* of information is crucial to our construct. The vast majority of Americans, for example, would agree that medical information is far more sensitive than name and address data. We want to protect privacy (avoid stigma, embarrassment, and the improper use or disclosure of personal information which robs the individual of a sense of security and trust), not anonymity. At the same time, we must keep in mind that in today's America, the price of admission—engaging in commerce, social intercourse, career, and reaping the benefits of such—is that we cannot masquerade, deny, change, or hide our identity.

- We should agree that the consensual model is best to the maximum degree possible, understanding that law enforcement and national security uses may outweigh getting prior consent for certain information. By this I mean that individuals should give permission (or not) at the time information is gathered and should agree to its use. Data should not be used for a different purpose unless new permission is obtained. However, we must recognize that public record data is, fundamentally, just that—public—and does not fit within the consensual model because of the current local, state and federal freedom of information acts.

- Everyone should have a right of access to data that is used to make decisions about them—subject to the same caveats about law enforcement and national security uses. In others words, expand the principles of the Fair Credit Reporting Act to all types of information: right to access, right to question the accuracy and prompt a review, and right to comment if a negative record is found to be accurate.

These basic approaches anchor the real privacy debate, a great cause to which I dedicate my efforts. It summons all of us, demands the best of us. Working together, logically, openly, without prejudice or preconception, we can create the constructs that safeguard our nation and the principles of liberty and human dignity on which it was founded.

PART VI

A CALL TO ACTION

In the small towns I've used as a metaphor for a less threatened America, the policeman extended society's sheltering arms into neighborhoods and homes. Experience enhanced his ability to do the job. Today, try explaining to a detective that it's not our jewelry that's been stolen, but our identity, and with it, our life savings. These kinds of assaults are outside the training, experience, and often the jurisdiction of the most determined investigator.

We cannot expect the government to attempt to mitigate many of the personal risks we're likely to encounter in our daily lives. As we'll see, information is or should be made available to help us quickly screen a nanny or verify that a prospective employee is not a wanted criminal.

Each of us plays a part in a network of interlocking responsibility that fits together like chain mail armor. Each of us must marshal information to shield our families, finances, homes, and communities. Businesses are charged with protecting their employees, customers, and investors from both economic and physical harm. It's vital that we make informed decisions when confronting these risks.

The "democratization of information" gives those of us with legitimate needs—parents; consumers; small businessmen and women; leaders of voluntary, religious, and social welfare organizations—access to data that can mitigate risk. This knowledge has enormous protective power, but it cannot be used in a vacuum. The chapters that follow argue that society must ensure that this power be tapped fairly, logically, effectively, and responsibly. But you must decide, if and how to put the positive power of information to work against your personal points of risk.

CHAPTER 22

Reducing Risk in Everyday Life

"Never send to know for whom the bell tolls; it tolls for thee."

JOHN DONNE

Ultimately, the information technologies we've discussed must empower the individual, because risk, like the funeral bell in John Donne's famous essay, shadows each of us every day of our lives. In 2004, the nature and velocity of risk make it impossible for the government or, for that matter, state and local law enforcement agencies, to mitigate the majority of threats in our daily lives. No policeman can *prevent* a Scout leader or priest from molesting my child. His job is to *solve* crimes. No consumer protection agency is going to directly advise me that the contractor I've hired to paint my house has a history of shoddy work and broken contracts unless I ask. No one is going to alert me to the fact that the surgeon operating on my mother trails a string of disciplinary actions and malpractice judgments. So wherever and whenever I can, I must shoulder this responsibility. I must step up to safeguard all that is valuable to me.

Our mobile, technology-driven society is the polar opposite of the safe and secure small-town paradigm. Risk, where it existed, was clear and identifiable. Today, we're confronted by an unforeseen, even unimagined peril: personal asymmetric risk. Sometimes the threat is physical; sometimes it's economic. Just as often, it's the death of innocence. You buy a computer so your children, whom you've nurtured and protected in every possible way, can e-mail their classmates and use the Internet to research homework assignments. And you find pornography in your son's room and a stranger stalking your daughter in a chat room. You don't know what to do or think or how to act. You find yourself, in your apartment, your secure suburb, or high-rise condominium with doorman and closed circuit surveillance cameras . . . helpless.

It's no exaggeration to say that for the last fifty years, most Americans lived in a vast, protective cocoon, confident that our lives, livelihood, and liberty were well-protected. Things have changed. To believe otherwise is to ignore the facts, or gamble that one person, family, or community can hide in the safety of numbers. Fortress America is no longer secure. Risk threatens us in many ways. Unchecked, it can call forth undemocratic responses: repressive legislation, vigilantism, demagoguery.

INTERLOCKING RESPONSIBILITIES

In Washington, the new threat matrix is forcing our leaders to focus more closely on global threats—terrorism, the spread of infectious disease, narcotics trafficking, nuclear proliferation. These issues are far beyond the reach of the individual or community. I can't do anything about terrorist training camps in Kashmir, opium poppy cultivation in Afghanistan, or cocaine factories in Bolivia. However, I can expect my government to act to confront these risks.

Every state government in the union has the same mission: protect the health, safety, and welfare of its citizens. But just as the role of the federal government is changing, so is how state—and even local—governments execute their duties.

State public safety agencies, for example, must continue to do what they do best: solve crimes and reduce risk by protecting us from predators and career criminals. However, many of the policies, regulations, and investigative processes that worked in the past almost certainly will not work today. Effective law enforcement demands new or updated skills, training, equipment, and laws to counter new risks such as identity theft and cyber crimes.

At the state level, information technologies like analytics and *iDNA* analysis are revolutionizing criminal investigations. New York's John Doe Project is an example of the marriage of justice and technology: medical examiners have begun to create *iDNA* profiles ("John Does") from rape kits and other biological evidence gathered at crime scenes. These profiles are being used in lieu of names to indict hundreds of unidentified assailants to get around the state's statute of limitations. This new form of indictment will extend New York's ability to hunt down vicious criminals who would otherwise escape punishment.

Apply the same concept more broadly and we may even call into question the need for a statute of limitations for crimes where technology can produce or preserve irrefutable evidence long after witnesses memories have failed.

In the small towns I've used as a metaphor for a less threatened

America, the policeman extended society's sheltering arms into neighborhoods and homes. In my town, the law was on a first-name basis with residents and shopkeepers. Policemen lived among us—their very presence deterred crime. Experience enhanced their ability to do their job: the misbehavior of teenage boys, burglars, or belligerent drunks was as predictable as the setting sun. In the case of a burglary, a detective would visit pawnshops in neighboring towns and take a hard look at the usual suspects. (They too were familiar figures.) More often than not, he'd come up with a perpetrator, and if you were lucky, your grandmother's engagement ring.

Try explaining to a detective burdened by a caseload of unsolved crimes, that it's not grandmother's ring that's been stolen, but her identity, and with it, her life savings, including money she's put away for her grandchildren's college education. When the officer asks for a description of the perpetrator, try explaining that the theft took place via the Internet, and as far as you can tell, the suspect lives on the other side of the country or maybe in Nigeria.

This kind of assault is outside the training, experience, and certainly, the jurisdiction of the most determined investigator. If a perpetrator is apprehended, the criminal justice system, not yet registering the virulence of identity-linked crime, will likely dispense a minimal sentence.

The new role of local police requires new or updated statutes and policies commensurate with the seriousness of these abuses. Next to an officer's handgun should be a holster for a PDA where they can wirelessly access data needed to solve crimes. Officers need training that counter the ease with which cyber criminals leap boundaries and borders.

There is an important corollary here: Changing roles mean I cannot expect (and, in most instances, do not want) the government to attempt to mitigate many of the risks I'm likely to encounter in my daily life. I'm not talking about apprehending criminals or maintaining the interstate highway system, but rather circumstances—screening a nanny or verifying a vendor's license—where available information enables me or the business community to do the job.

Personal asymmetric risk cannot be deflected by gated communities and neighborhood patrols. Each of us plays a part in a network of interlocking responsibility that fits together like chain mail armor. The federal government operates on the global stage. Local law enforcement keeps our communities safe using the right mix of traditional and information age tactics. We, as individuals, must now marshal information to shield our families, finances, homes, and communities. Businesses are charged with protecting their employees, customers, and investors from both economic and physical harm.

In the past, all of us made high-risk decisions based largely on gut feelings—"instincts"—and the guidance (referrals and recommendations) of family and neighbors. Today, that support system is fading. Yet it is vital that we make *informed* decisions: we can still trust, but we must also verify. Today, we're witnessing the "democratization of information," an evolution that gives individuals with legitimate needs—parents; consumers; small businessmen and women; leaders of voluntary, religious, and social welfare organizations—access to data that can mitigate risk. This knowledge has enormous protective power, but it cannot be used in a vacuum. As we've seen, to move forward, society must craft *decision rules* allowing this power to be tapped fairly, logically, effectively, and responsibly.

To better illustrate how decision rules might work for us on a personal level, I've chosen two areas where the inability to access (or awareness of) available information has consistently had tragic consequences. The first is medical malpractice information. The second involves the screening of volunteers and others in whom society invests enormous trust. I've also selected two areas where information technology is having a tremendously positive impact: the recovery of missing and kidnapped children and the interdiction of Internet predators. I use these examples because I'm most familiar with them and because these stories are excellent illustrations of how we must take more personal responsibility for acting on the risk in our lives.

CHAPTER 23

Stopping Dangerous Doctors

In the past, a license, a board certification, a referral from a trusted friend seemed a reliable indicator of a medical practitioner's competence. As health care evolved from local practitioner and community clinic to a multibillion dollar industry, its seemed prudent to assume that a doctor's employer—the hospital, group, HMO, etc.—would monitor her professional competence. In a small town setting, an egregiously incompetent surgeon, for example, would see her referrals and her practice wither.

THE ANONYMITY OF THE WHITE COAT

Today, though, an incompetent or outright dangerous health-care practitioner can simply walk away, relocate to another city, and afflict a new round of patients cloaked by the anonymity of the white coat and stethoscope. How serious is the problem? The National Academy of Sciences' Institute of Medicine predicts that in 2004, 98,000 Americans will die because of mistakes made by medical practitioners, a figure twice as large as the number who'll perish in automobile accidents.

One of every seven doctors in the United States—*more than 14 percent of those now practicing*—has a malpractice settlement or disciplinary action in his or her files. More than 20,000 physicians around the country have had their professional skills labeled "questionable" by Public Citizen, a not-for-profit watchdog group.

These statistics do not reflect bad luck or inevitability. These are deaths and injuries at the hands of physicians who typically hide their histories of malpractice.

Information is available to help mitigate the risk, stored in legal filings, state archives, and an online federal National Practitioner Data Bank (NPDB) containing disciplinary reports, license revocations, and records of some $25 billion in malpractice settlements involving more than 146,000 doctors and dentists. This database contains significant information searchable, predictive, and one would imagine, in the public domain. However, the National Practitioner Data Bank, maintained at taxpayer expense, is off-limits to consumers—a nod, however cynical, to a medical professional's right to privacy.

UNCOVERING A COVERUP

Since 2000, ABC News, the *Hartford Courant* and a handful of other news organizations have plumbed the National Practitioner Data Bank uncovering what can only be called a massive coverup. ABC's *20/20* newsmagazine shocked millions of viewers with the stories of Paul Young and Willie King.

In 1995, attending physicians assured Paul Young, a grocery store manager in Alvarado, Texas, that the surgery he'd undergone to repair a stomach ulcer had been a complete success. Despite the assurances, Young suffered excruciating abdominal pain in the aftermath of the operation. Pain none of his doctors could alleviate or explain. He suffered for five years, passing through the offices of half-a-dozen specialists along the way. Finally, an X-ray confirmed that the original surgical team had neglected to remove a thirteen-inch steel retractor from his abdomen.

A one-in-a-million occurrence? Hardly. The federal Centers for Disease Control and Prevention (CDC) estimates that in the last five years, 15,000 people have had foreign objects left in their bodies after undergoing surgical procedures. In Paul Young's case, it turned out that the understaffed surgical team had no instrument-counting procedure. (In an attempt to cut costs, hospital administrators had replaced a veteran operating room nurse with an inexperienced technician.) That's information patients about to undergo surgery at the facility might have found enlightening.

In Mr. Young's case, at least four decision rules can be applied:

- **Decision Rule 1:** *Identify the risk* that foreign objects could be left behind during surgery. Based on the publicly available CDC statistics, the risk is real.

- **Decision Rule 2 & 3:** *Determine what legitimate information exists to reduce the risk.* Is there information about the hospital, surgeon, and surgery team members that relates to the risk? The answer is yes. The NPDB and the hospital's own records would show the history and experience of the surgeon and operating room team.

• **Decision Rule 4:** *Determine who is allowed access and who sets decision criteria.* Information about the surgeon and team was not accessible by Mr. Young a decision made by government officials.

These circumstances combine to yield Decision Result 1: Significant negative consequences, primarily because of the lack of open access to valuable data about the experience level of the surgical team and the hospital's OR procedures.

ABC News also highlighted the case of Willy King, a man who was admitted to a Tampa, Florida, hospital to have his right leg amputated. King awoke to discover his left leg removed. A freak accident? Hardly. Since 1997, an estimated 50,000 individuals have filed "wrong site" lawsuits against physicians and hospitals. It turned out that the surgeon who'd botched the King procedure had mistakenly amputated a woman's toe and, along the way, had implanted a central catheter into a patient not scheduled for the procedure. Florida's Board of Medicine considers this information off-limits to the public.

In this case, four decision rules combined to lead to a result—a very negative one for Mr. King:

• **Decision Rule 1:** *Identify the risk* in the having the medical procedure performed by the physician, at the hospital selected. Generic statistics show "wrong site" surgical mistakes are not uncommon.

• **Decision Rule 2 & 3:** *Determine what legitimate information* *exists to reduce the risk.* Specific information about the physician shows at least two serious surgical errors similar to the one ultimately suffered by Mr. King.

• **Decision Rule 4:** *Determine who is allowed access and who sets decision criteria* regarding information about Mr. King's physician. Health-care consumers cannot access the information, based on federal law.

Information existed that would have allowed Mr. King to make a more informed decision about his physician selection, but because he was not allowed access, he could not assess the true risks of the procedure. The outcome, Decision Result 1: Significant negative consequence for all involved.

"FIRST, DO NO HARM"

The worst of the horror stories are true. It's also true that *the overwhelming majority of medical practitioners are skilled and caring individuals.* For that reason alone, it's in the best interest of responsible and caring physicians as well as the public that these irresponsible few be exposed before more harm is done. But the truth is, hundreds, even thousands of malpractice filings remain hidden from the public eye.

In 2000, Congressman Tom Bliley of Virginia, then chairman of the House Commerce Committee, introduced legislation to create a website giving consumers access to physicians' malpractice histories. Bliley captured the need for such a service succinctly: "Most consumers are forced to choose a doctor from a list of providers or even the Yellow Pages, doctors they might know next to nothing about," he said. "The

American public currently has more comparative information about the used car we purchase or the snack food we eat, than the doctors in whose care we entrust our health and well-being."

At a September 2000 hearing held to build support for the legislation, a Californian named Ruben Fernandez told the House Commerce Committee that his wife's death—she succumbed after a botched cosmetic surgery procedure—was the result of her inability to access her surgeon's disciplinary history. A history that included four malpractice judgments. Bliley's legislation—the Patient Protection Act of 2000—also succumbed.

The NPDB remains accessible to insurance companies, hospitals, federal and state regulators, but not the public, violating Decision Result 2: Prudent behaviors will emerge. In this case, there is no clear standard of prudent behavior that favors those who could benefit most. One positive development: the database has been opened, with restrictions, to the media, who, the thinking goes, will cover the worst offenders.

Hippocrates' phrase, "First, do no harm," is a fundamental principle of medicine. Under the weight of the kind of embarrassments discussed here, the medical establishment has begun to realize that making performance data public poses no threat to the overwhelming majority of health-care providers. This is the realization of Decision Rule 3: Determine the legitimacy of available information. Ensuring the application of information against the identified risk actually reduces the risk. In fact, putting malpractice records online, with proper safeguards, is not only in the public interest, it's in the best interests of competent and qualified professionals. What happens then is Decision Result 2: Prudent behaviors will emerge.

This sea change is underway in the states. Over the objections of the Massachusetts Medical Society, the state created the first online physicians profiling system in 1996. The database contains doctors' names, addresses, medical education, board certification, along with disciplinary actions and criminal convictions. Other states, most recently Georgia and Washington, have followed suit, modeling their offerings (with some modifications) on the Massachusetts' model. Georgia's database lists felony convictions, malpractice settlements, and disciplinary actions. New York's database cites hospital restrictions, criminal convictions, and malpractice information.

Compromises on what information goes into these databases can soothe physicians' concerns. Virginia's database carries disclaimers. California requires that malpractice settlements be posted only for doctors who chalk up three or more $150,000-plus judgments in a ten-year period (more in certain high-risk specialties)—a stipulation many physicians agreed was reasonable. All of these statutes are attempts to implement Decision Rule 3: Determine the legitimacy of available information.

"Did it cause doctors to flee the state?" Nancy Achin Audesse, executive director of the Massachusetts Board of Registration in Medicine, remarked to a reporter for the AMA's *American Medical News* in May 2003. "The answer is no. This is supposed to be a consumer education tool. No doctor should be afraid of good patient information."

The bottom line is quite simple: we must take personal responsibility for assessing the quality of physicians and health-care facilities. We must seek out the information that can help reduce risks that come from selecting the wrong health-care provider. If denied access, we must demand the information be shared so an informed decision can be made.

CHAPTER 24

Targeting Sex Offenders

Few tragedies can compare to the abuses suffered by our children because available information on known sexual predators was ignored or overlooked. There are lessons about personal responsibility to be learned here, too.

For nearly two hundred years, the First Baptist Church in Columbia, South Carolina, has been one of the pillars of the state's capital. With a 5,500-member congregation, the church sponsors dozens of outstanding community outreach programs, youth camps, Scout troops, Sunday school, prison and overseas ministries. Today, First Baptist's congregation and its pastor, Rev. Wendell Estep, are trying to recover from the worst kind of tragedy, focusing much of their energy and resources on criminal allegations, lawsuits, and community outrage rather than good works and spiritual concerns.

THE TRAP OF UNAWARENESS

The chaos was triggered by that foul and familiar crime, child abuse, committed by a former church deacon and youth volunteer named John Hubner. As with so many individuals, businesses, and community groups, First Baptist's leaders fell into the trap of being unaware of the risks around them, ignorant of the facts and statistics that show how often children are targeted by those who would steal their innocence. According to the U.S. Department of Justice, 78 percent of all victims of sex crimes are under eighteen. One of every three girls and one of every five boys will be the victim of sexual abuse by an adult. More than 25 percent of those now incarcerated will be rearrested for similar crimes upon being released into the community.

John Hubner arrived in South Carolina in the early 1990s. Married, with two daughters, to all appearances an upstanding individual, Hubner began attending First Baptist services in 1992 and was soon among the congregation's most active members (a perfectly camouflaged asymmetric threat). He became a church deacon, a volunteer in church youth programs, including Sunday school, the Boy Scout troop, and the Baptism Committee. "If he was good enough to be a deacon, he was good enough to teach Sunday school," Tad Wilson, a former youth minister would later tell reporters Rick Brundrett and Allison Askins who covered the scandal for *The State* newspaper. "He was the kind of guy that if you asked him to do something, he'd do it."

What Hubner was careful not to do, was inform church officials that he had pleaded guilty to charges of unlawful sexual conduct with a twelve-year-old girl in Maine in 1983. Hubner was originally charged with the rape of two girls. This was information documented in criminal records and sex offender registries available to anyone, including

First Baptist, who wished to check.

Church officials would learn soon enough. In January 2001, Hubner was indicted for sexually assaulting a twelve-year-old on six different occasions; five of the assaults took place in the South Carolina church's annex. Hubner maintained his innocence even as evidence continued to emerge. In September 2002, he was convicted on all counts and sentenced to thirty-six years in prison.

According to a civil lawsuit filed against First Baptist, the church had received written and verbal complaints from parents about Hubner's "unnatural interest in their young sons and daughters" as early as 1996. Nonetheless, Hubner continued as deacon and Scout leader for five more years.

The lawsuit held the church responsible because they'd violated "duty of care" responsibilities by failing to do a background check that would have turned up Hubner's criminal history. Specifically, the suit alleged they'd ignored "the risk posed by allowing a convicted child sex offender to volunteer to work with the church's youth."

As part of an out-of-court settlement, First Baptist agreed to establish a counseling referral service for sex abuse victims; continue to seek out others who may have been victimized by Hubner; and conduct abuse awareness seminars for parents and children. In June 2001, the church had begun screening all its volunteers and agreed to support legislation—since passed by the South Carolina legislature—requiring religious institutions to report any incident of sexual misconduct involving children to the authorities.

None of these eminently reasonable policies was in place when John Hubner had access to the church's most vulnerable and innocent wards. Rev. Estep told *The State* newspaper "in my thirty-two years of ministry this is the first time a situation like this has occurred." He was speaking from the heart, struggling to accept that evil could flourish among so much good. A warning endlessly repeated in the Scriptures, but rarely heeded.

The lesson we learn from the grievous pain and suffering of the children, families, and the church itself is that decision rules and the taking of personal responsibility apply to institutions as well as individuals. In this case:

- **Decision Rule 1:** *Identify the risk* to children from known sexual offenders. Overwhelming evidence exists that shows where children gather, so do sexual predators.

- **Decision Rule 2 & 3:** *Determine what legitimate information exists to reduce the risk* about known sexual offenders. Public records and sexual offender registries provide a means to reduce the risks.

- **Decision Rule 4:** *Determine who is allowed access and who sets decision criteria* that will allow the church to assess and reduce the risk. With few exceptions, criminal records are available to the public, often times online. In this case, the church would set the decision criteria used to determine if a person is hired or allowed to volunteer to work with children.

- **Decision Result 2:** *Prudent behaviors will emerge.* In this case, the required screening of volunteers who work with children, regardless of the person's standing in the community.

CRIMINAL VOLUNTEERS

As much as we all would like for the Huber case to be an isolated one, the fact is, such outrages are a daily occurrence, staggering in number, amazing in their virulence.

In 2003, a national survey done by *Volunteer Select* revealed that more than 15,000 out of approximately 460,000 individuals seeking to volunteer for youth, senior citizen, disabled, and other community programs had undisclosed criminal records. That's a felony "hit rate" of a little more than 3 percent.

The rap sheets include murder and manslaughter convictions, assaults, thousands of drug and alcohol offenses, along with thousands of thefts and burglaries. Would-be volunteers had been convicted of rape, child abuse, and other sex offenses. In one case, a man with eight child molestation convictions was seeking access to young people just two months after his release from jail.

Who were the victims? I can tell you that forty-one of the laws violated by the thousands of applicants included the word "minor" in their descriptions. In a world of escalating and unexpected risk, naiveté and blind trust open the door to the enemy.

THE CLOAK OF ANONYMITY

The scandal that rocked First Baptist Church in South Carolina is part of an ugly stain spreading across the fabric of religious and community life, undermining the faith and trust of millions of believers. In Wisconsin, the Church Mutual Insurance Company now advises the 76,000 churches, camps, and senior living facilities it insures do background screening on all staff members, particularly volunteers who come in contact with children.

After years of inaction, the Catholic church is now moving aggressively to staunch its problems. It's now deploying technology to reduce the risk of continued abuse by priests, teachers, volunteers, and other individuals associated with or employed by the church.

The cloak of anonymity behind which these twisted people are hidden can be removed swiftly and effectively. For example, a confidential database containing sensitive records on sanctioned clergy or lay people would be a great leap forward in reducing the risk of repeat offenders. Operating on a desktop computer, it would allow information sharing among widely scattered dioceses, prevent the hiring of individuals, who, by past behavior or criminal history, represent a risk no religious organization should tolerate. The database would be accessible only to those with legitimate authority. It would incorporate state-of-the-art safeguards.

Such as system would incorporate Decision Rule 2, 3 & 4: Determine information exists, determine the legitimacy of available information, and determine who is allowed access and who sets decision criteria to ensure the appropriate results. Decision Results 1 & 2: Significant positive consequences, and prudent behaviors will emerge. The template already exists. What is missing is the will.

Though painful, the pervasiveness of child abuse can be a catalyst for positive change. In the fall of 2002, the U.S. Senate passed the National Child Protection Improvement Act, legislation authored by Senators Joe Biden of Delaware and the late Strom Thurmond of South Carolina. The bill authorized $100 million to fund a Justice Department clearinghouse providing criminal background checks to nonprofit organizations—a great step in the right direction. Eighteen months later, the legislation was still on hold, yielding Decision Result 1: Negative consequences.

In an exercise of personal responsibility (or in this case corporate responsibility), businesses and nonprofit organizations have come together to tackle an issue the government has, to date, failed to address. In April 2002, the Boys & Girls Clubs of America, which operates 3,000 facilities serving 3.3 million children across the country, began screening its volunteers. In October 2002, Little League baseball announced its one million volunteers would henceforth be run against sex offender databases. Pop Warner football (37,000 volunteers) quickly followed suit, as did the American Red Cross, Girls Scouts of the USA, Campfire USA, 4H Clubs and Big Brothers Big Sisters of America. The Boy Scouts of America (more than one million volunteers) and U.S. Youth Soccer (60,000 volunteers) issued their recommendations on how to screen adult volunteers in 2003.

These organizations, by design or happenstance, have followed each step of the decision rule matrix, including the creation of a standard of prudent behavior and a positive consequence: a more secure environment for the children in their charge.

CHAPTER 25

Finding Missing Children

Two thousand children are reported missing in the United States each day. That translates to some 750,000 annually, an extraordinary burden on distraught families, social services agencies, and the law enforcement officers expected to bring these kids home safely. The majority involve runaways, but abductions by family members, typically divorced parents enraged by custodial or child support conflicts, are the second most common abduction at 200,000 each year. In some of these cases, children born to foreign nationals and American spouses are spirited out of the country. In others, a noncustodial parent will transport a child across state lines, in effect, disappearing into a fog of 281 million strangers.

Nonfamily members abduct 58,000 children each year. Sexual predators take a tiny fraction of that number, but half of these will be murdered. The good news is that information is being marshaled to protect these children. For nearly fifteen years, the National Center for Missing and Exploited Children (NCMEC) has deployed ever more sophisticated technologies (from pictures on milk cartons to direct mail, computer imaging, broadcast faxing, e-mail, and the World Wide Web) in its efforts to recover lost and at-risk youth. There has been a dramatic increase in positive outcomes in these cases, in no small part due to information technology advances. (Decision Result 1: Significant positive consequences of the considered decision to use information for good.)

The critical time in the search for a missing child is the first few hours following a disappearance. Seventy-four percent of abducted children who are murdered are killed within three hours of disappearing. One such crime took place in Concord, New Hampshire, on the evening of July 4, 2003. Townspeople at a holiday fireworks display noticed a local accountant named Manuel Gehring raging at his two children as he drove away from the celebration. The proximate cause of Gehring's anger was that fourteen year-old Sarah and her boyfriend had arrived late to the festivities, but his rage sprung from a deeper well. For months, Gehring had been feuding with his ex-wife, Teresa, over where Sarah and eleven-year-old Philip should live in the aftermath of the couple's divorce. An agreement was reached earlier in the summer allowing the children to split time between the parents. Gehring reneged.

He disappeared that holiday evening, heading, as he later told investigators, for the West Coast. Gehring would insist that he'd dropped the children off at his apartment and drove alone to California. Six days later, in Gilroy, California, FBI agents searched Gehring's van. They found bullet holes covered by duct tape, shell fragments, blood and tissue, but no bodies. Under questioning, Gehring broke down, confessing he'd murdered his children on the side of a road forty-five minutes from Concord, a time-span precisely in line with NCMEC statistics.

Such tragedies give lie to the assumption that family abductions are not serious matters. Tens of thousands of children are living fugitive lives, stripped of parents' love and guidance, ripped away from homes, school, family, and friends. Inexorably, information technologies are turning up more and more of these at-risk kids. In 1989, NCMEC was able to recover 66 percent of the children being sought. Today, the figure is 94 percent, a phenomenal demonstration of the positive power of information technology.

HIGH-TECH RISKS/HIGH-TECH RESPONSES

According to a recent NCMEC survey (conducted by the University of New Hampshire's Crimes Against Children Research Center), one in five children aged ten to seventeen who frequent Internet chat rooms is accosted by sexual predators. Five percent of those surveyed reported a "distressing sexual solicitation." Three percent said they'd received an "aggressive solicitation involving offline contact or attempts at offline contact." The seriousness of these assaults cannot be downplayed—we're talking about millions of our children.

Given the fantasies, emotional turmoil, grievances, longings, and imaginings swirling in youthful psyches, many of these children become easy prey for manipulating adults. In Louisville, Kentucky, federal agents and members of a taskforce targeting Internet sexual predators spent months posing as a fourteen-year-old girl who liked to frequent chat rooms, an example of law enforcement gearing up to meet new demands and challenges.

Online, the virtual "child" drew sexual attention the way chum draws sharks. Taskforce members used e-mail–tracing technology to identify the most egregious solicitations from men who imagined themselves safely hidden in their digital guise. By the winter of 2002, nine individuals had been indicted for soliciting sex with a minor. Some also faced charges of crossing state lines for sex with a minor. Six entered guilty pleas. At the beginning of 2004, criminal proceedings were underway against the others.

One of the most disturbing aspects of this case was that few of those charged fit the stereotype of the sexual predator: a leering, dysfunctional loser. Kevin Hamm, of Mount Laurel, New Jersey, who pleaded guilty, was the CEO of an Internet company. Hamm was arrested in Baltimore after wiring money for an airline ticket that would ferry the girl to him. John Paine, sentenced to two years in prison, operated a string of veterinary clinics in Indianapolis. What the Louisville investigation revealed is hardly unique; it's another reminder that technology *must be used* to offset the very abuses it can enable. These were men emboldened by the anonymity of the Internet, respectable individuals who would never have dared approach a child in a town park or city neighborhood.

Whether it's more parental involvement or technologies that prevent visits to risky websites, it is our personal responsibility to take the actions necessary to protect our children. As we'll see, others may help us, but they cannot fulfill our duties.

CODE ADAM

I've already outlined how we all must take more responsibility for our own security. Such personal responsibility is not limited to individuals, or even volunteer groups. The role of the business community is changing, too.

While I've argued that small-town culture has faded, Code Adam, a child recovery program sponsored by the retail community, can be seen as a high-tech extension of the cop on the beat or the vigilant shopkeeper who "kept an eye" on neighborhood kids in the 1950s and 1960s. A beat cop is almost impossible to find and the neighborhood store has, for the most part, given way to a shopping mall. The good news is that the cop now has (or soon will have) a laptop in his cruiser and a PDA device on his gun belt. Retail giants like Wal-Mart, K Mart, Shop Rite, and Kroger have taken the place of the shopkeeper in the community watch program.

Wal-Mart launched Code Adam in 1994. The program grew out of a searing tragedy. It is named for Adam Walsh, the six-year-old son of John Walsh, NCMEC co-founder and "America's Most Wanted" host. Adam was abducted from a department store (not Wal-Mart) in Hollywood, Florida, in 1981. The kidnapping took place while Reve Walsh, Adam's mother, shopped for lamps seventy-five feet away. (Adam was in the toy department watching a group of older children play a video game.) Years later, Reve Walsh would recall rushing frantically through the store searching for the child while clerks and customers went blandly about their business. Every exit was unguarded; there were no alert mechanisms, no alarms to sound.

"Oh, he probably just wandered off," people's refrain pierced Walsh's despairing heart like a dagger. *"You know how kids are."* For sixteen days, the city was flooded with door-to-door canvassers carrying pictures of a little boy with a baseball cap and gap-tooth smile. And then everyone's worst fears were realized. A severed head was discovered, the horror of Adam Walsh's death confirmed. Through years of investigation, through suspect lists and hundreds of tips, despite John Walsh's never-ending efforts, no one has ever been indicted for killing Adam Walsh.

If any good can come out of tragedy, Adam Walsh has made such a nightmare less likely. Across the nation, 45,000 stores and supermarkets now participate in the Code Adam program in which an alert is announced over a store's public address system when a child is reported missing in that store. A description of the missing child is transmitted to designated employees who begin searching; other employees monitor exits. If the child is not found in ten minutes or if the child is observed accompanied by someone other than the parent or guardian, the police are summoned. At that point, the search expands to other stores, malls, and parking facilities—even roadblocks and car by car searches. In October 2002, Code Adam foiled a kidnapping at a Crawfordsville, Indiana, Wal-Mart. A man, who turned out to have a history of child abduction, was arrested at the scene, later convicted, and taken off the streets. That month, in Pascagoula, Mississippi, the protocol sped the hunt for and, a day later, the recovery of a seven-year-old who disappeared while her parents shopped.

ADAM alerts, another private sector-driven child-recovery system, expands the reach of Code Adam beyond the retail outlet or shopping mall. ADAM alerts have been particularly effective in marshaling information to track runaways and family abductions. ADAM alerts hone in on specific geographic areas (designated by zip codes) where the child is likely to have traveled, been taken, or has been sighted. Using data-based longitude and latitude coordinates (geocoding), faxes, e-mail, and other wireless messaging systems, ADAM administrators bracket police, news media, schools, businesses, medical centers, and other institutions in the target area with posters and images. In a 2002 partnership, Yahoo! expanded ADAM's reach by putting the alerts online. Radio Shack added its thousands of retail locations to the ADAM alert network in 2003.

DOES IT WORK? ABSOLUTELY

A sixteen-year-old runaway reported missing in St. Louis, Missouri, in September 2001, was recovered months later, after an e-mail she sent to her mother was traced to a San Francisco library. ADAM directed faxed images of the teen to businesses and community organizations near the library. She turned up in a homeless shelter. In the spring of 2002, information and photos of a fourteen-year-old missing from Columbus, Ohio, were faxed to Beckley, West Virginia, where it was determined she might have traveled to join her mother. One of the faxes arrived at Woodrow Wilson High School. School administrators found her among a group of new enrollees.

All told, nearly 100 missing or exploited children have been returned to their loved ones since 2000 as a result of ADAM—proof that the private sector is taking seriously its role in the new community watch. But even more can be done when you equip one last player to the effort to keep our children safe.

CHAPTER 26

Empowering the Individual

At a time when it is vital that each of us—to the extent we can—create a safer society, technology grants us that power. Here's a perfect example: in the summer of 2003, a child abduction warning flashed to startled motorists traveling west on Interstate 285 outside Atlanta. The warning, on an electronic billboard ordinarily used to communicate travel advisories, gave a description of a late-model car that police were hunting. In moments, thousands of energized drivers had joined the search. This particular alert was part of the AMBER plan, a voluntary partnership between law enforcement, highway transportation agencies, and broadcasters used in the most serious child abduction cases.

Like Code Adam, the AMBER system grew out of a tragedy. In 1996, nine-year-old Amber Hagerman was murdered after being kidnapped while riding her bicycle in Arlington, Texas, near Dallas. Outrage at the murder prompted the city to devise a system tapping local radio stations to broadcast emergency alerts—much like those flashed for severe weather warnings—to galvanize a community after an abduction.

AMBER alerts must meet certain criteria. Police must confirm a child has been abducted; there must be reason to believe the child is in mortal danger (remember the statistic about most abducted children are killed within a short time frame). There must be sufficient descriptive evidence about the child, suspect, or suspect's vehicle to determine that broadcasting an alert may save a life. The alert is then relayed by the major broadcast outlets in an area to radio, television, and cable stations via the Emergency Broadcast System. In the Atlanta incident described above, technology piggybacked the alarm onto electronic highway billboards, a dramatic leap forward in the race against the clock.

AMBER is, in a sense, Nirvana: government agencies, the private sector, and individuals—linked by technology, armed with information—exercising their new roles dictated by the changing risk environment in which we live.

THE EDGE OF THE ENVELOPE

In the spring of 2002, Jeffrey, Leslie, and Derek Jacobs became the first American family to get "chipped." As TV news crews and reporters watched, a physician made a tiny incision, then used an oversized needle to implant a VeriChip, a microprocessor the size of a rice grain into the arm of each family member. The procedure took ten seconds, more than enough time for the Florida family to be christened "The Chipsons," after the family in the futuristic cartoon series "The Jetsons." The device, developed by Applied Digital Systems, stores an

ID number that, in the case of accident or emergency, can be scanned and uplinked to a database containing health-care information on each family member. (It's designed to store more extensive medical history data, subject to governmental approval.) Upcoming models feature GPS capabilities allowing, for example, kidnapped or missing children and Alzheimer's patients to be tracked and located instantaneously.

Despite all the media attention, the Jacobs' decision was an attempt to mitigate a very real risk: Jeffery Jacobs is battling Hodgkins disease. If he becomes unconscious or incapacitated, he told ABC News, the chip would provide instant, electronic access to his medical history and his long list of medications—saving time and maybe his life. "It's a great feeling," he said. "I have more sense of security."

When I first learned of the Jacobs family, I was threatened. Taken to an extreme—a government mandate for example—getting chipped is repugnant and should never be contemplated, let alone allowed. Yet, as I learned more about why Mr. Jacobs had the chip implanted, I began to believe that he, too, had followed the decision rule matrix in the ultimate display of personal responsibility.

• **Decision Rule 1:** *Identify the risk.* Mr. Jacobs suffers from a potentially debilitating disease and may not be able to communicate the information to health-care professionals in an emergency. That's a significant and real risk.

• **Decision Rule 2 & 3:** *Determine what legitimate information exists to reduce the risk.* In this case, legitimate medical information is available to help mitigate the risk of not being able to communicate with medical personnel, without creating an unintended negative consequence for others. The Jacobs family clearly believes having vital medical informa-

tion immediately available in the form of an implant miti-
gates any risk. And, since the Jacobs decision is completely
voluntary, it has no impact on anyone else.

• **Decision Rule 4:** *Determine who is allowed access and who
sets decision criteria.* This falls completely within the control
of the Jacobs. They have access to their own information and
they control who else has access.

Bottom line: Decision Result 1: Significant positive consequences
for the Jacobs family in the form of peace of mind and access to medical information in an emergency.

Getting chipped is an extreme measure that is not for everyone.
Yet, how we attempt to reduce risk is less important than the fact that
all of us must take responsibility for reducing the risk in our lives and
the lives of our loved ones. The Jacobs selected what was best for them,
and for that, they deserve our praise.

Even the most advanced technology, however, is merely a stopgap
measure. As we'll see, enormous global challenges must be confronted if
we are to restore and protect what is good both at home and in the world
at large. That struggle is about hearts and minds, not technologies.

PART VII

A BIG-PICTURE PERSPECTIVE

Technology alone cannot solve the deep-rooted problems plaguing our country and the world. Information can be misunderstood, misapplied, or worse, assigned powers or responsibilities beyond its reach. Those of us trying to blunt the terrors of the Risk Revolution understand that in much of the world, technology can mitigate, but never eliminate the suffering and the risk created by poverty and social decay. The implications and obligations created by that awareness are covered in the final four chapters that conclude this book. In particular, "The Limits of Technology" expands my focus beyond the available and appropriate uses of information to root causes and global concerns, seemingly intractable issues. Issues, however, that must be addressed thoughtfully and humanely if our world is truly to become safer and more secure. Each time in our nation's history when we have faced a particularly daunting challenge, we have embraced it, conquered it, and emerged stronger from the experience. It is this fundamental optimism that makes our country unique in the world and it is what convinces me we will create a better world for ourselves and our children.

CHAPTER 27

The Limits of Technology

On the morning of September 10th, 2003, an unnerving story surfaced in the media, then quickly disappeared among accounts of Middle East violence and commemorations marking the anniversary of the September 11th attacks. The story described how a shipping clerk named Charles McKinley literally had himself crated and shipped from New York to Dallas in the belly of a cargo plane. The "homesick" McKinley, arrested on unrelated charges after being delivered to his parents' house, told reporters that he'd gotten out of his crate while airborne and strolled around the hold of the airplane. It doesn't require a leap of the imagination to imagine the havoc a terrorist loose on that transport could have wreaked. When you consider that our government has spent $9 billion to beef up airport security using sophisticated "bomb-sniffing" machines and other cutting-edge devices, it's incredible this kind of vulnerability still exists.

NO MAGIC BULLET

The McKinley story illustrates a fundamental truth about technology, a fact ignored to our peril: *it is not a magic bullet*. One man on a mission, however absurd, essentially negated billions of dollars invested and the best minds in the security industry. If we expand that focus, it becomes clear that technology alone cannot solve the deep-rooted problems plaguing our country and the rest of the world. It also becomes obvious that information can be misunderstood, misapplied, or worse, assigned powers or responsibilities beyond its reach. Those of us living on the edge of the Risk Revolution understand that technology can mitigate, but never eliminate, the suffering and the risk created by poverty and social decay. The implications and obligations created by that awareness are covered in this chapter.

I've argued that information can help restore the sense of well-being many Americans associate with small-town life in the 1950s and early 1960s—a moment in history when the storms of change that would transform the world were first beginning to mass. I chose that period for reasons other than the fact that it represents the time and place I came of age. Societies are organic; over time, they expand and contract, mature and decay. They manifest characteristics that in many cases are imprinted by stimulus, experience, and history. Who can deny that American society has changed dramatically in the last forty years? Who can look to Russia, the Middle East, or the Pacific Rim without seeing momentous upheavals which continue to accelerate?

In my view, the small-town metaphor can be applied anytime and anywhere a circumscribed community or belief system—be it religious, ethnic, or cultural—is challenged by outside forces beyond its control.

Today, the barbarians pounding the gates of the developing world are not marauding hordes, but a subtler invader marching under the banner of communications, modernization, and globalization. Technology is driving this assault, creating greater and greater levels of angst among threatened peoples, religious groups, and cultures.

Backed into a corner, the human impulse is to strike back, often blindly. For the first time in history, a minority culture or belief system that is (or perceives itself) threatened has the *speed and the ability* to retaliate in kind, to wreak massive physical and psychological havoc on its tormentor. Nineteen terrorists were able to inspire more fear and uncertainty among Americans than Hitler's or Tojo's hordes ever did. As Loyola University professor John Allen Williams phrased it, western societies are in the remarkable position of being threatened by men living in caves, by men and women willing to embrace suicide to commit homicide—capable, even eager to use weapons of mass destruction against us.

Whether you experienced small-town life or grew up in a mobile, less rooted America, small towns still symbolize familiar faces, safe schools and churches, protective communities. More than financial success, freedom and security represent the American Dream, but also humanity's dream. Yet the hope for a safe haven has been so often dashed throughout history.

Certainly, the fog of memory renders those small American towns perfect, as idealized as the black and white photos in *Life* magazine, as solid and reliable as a gray flannel suit. They were not. Colors were brighter; contrasts more strident. Poverty, racial injustice, and other inequities cast a deep shadow over society—as they do today—but these ills, to use a modern phrase, were *inside the box*. Most Americans were confident social problems would be addressed—as the Depression, malnutrition, and infectious diseases like polio and smallpox had been addressed—by right-thinking people pulling together toward a common goal, inspired by a common destiny. Terrorism, biological warfare, and religious fanaticism were *way outside the box*, metastasizing threats that demand new ideas and approaches.

THE ACCELERATING THREAT

In the past, such threats called forth simple solutions: speed has been America's great advantage. In second half of the twentieth century, we were consistently faster to war, faster to market, faster to leap into the Information Age. In World War II, the great private/public sector alliance that turned the United States into the greatest war machine in history, offsetting Pearl Harbor and the Third Reich's decade-long preparation for war. More recently, the advantage America gained by launching the personal computer is incalculable.

Quickness can hold risk at bay until policy, a much slower and more convoluted process, catches up. But the democratization of technology has stripped away America's advantage. Speed, our ally, has now become a threat. The destructive power of an entire army or a nuclear warhead can be wielded by a handful of determined men. Speed and technology now cede advantage to our enemies, be they international terrorists or homegrown criminals. They have the tools. They don't worry about policy implications. We must. They act. We hesitate while the clock ticks. The bottom line: if effective policy is not forthcoming at this high-risk historical moment, we will lose.

The impact of another mass casualty assault on our homeland will not be measured in lost lives and economic havoc. It will quickly birth an environment so paranoid and security-conscious that our democratic freedoms will almost certainly be abridged. In the corridors of power, the slow and judicious debate that has kept our democracy unabridged for two centuries is now too slow and less than judicious. This is the asymmetric threat come full circle. This is how we lose.

CHAPTER 28

The Roots of Conflict

Effective and coherent policymaking is based on a simple fact: without context, information is a meaningless string of digits and bytes. In the nineteenth century, "Wanted" posters circulated across the Old West by stagecoach and Pony Express. The information— rewards, descriptions, aliases, etc.—helped bring bank robbers and cattle rustlers to justice, but it didn't dissuade many outlaws from committing crimes. Those roots ran deeper: disgruntled Civil War veterans continued to scavenge and plunder; law officers and courts were few and far between; disenfranchised cowboys and sodbusters driven from ranches and farms drifted anonymously from one territory to another. Each of these circumstances was unique; together they demanded a set of solutions that entailed more than calling in the cavalry. Law and order were needed certainly, but also land, opportunity, and justice.

A century later, during the Vietnam War, the Pentagon used "body counts" (number of enemy killed in action) to measure success—an ill-conceived measure against an adversary willing to assume massive casualties to achieve victory. It was a strategy that ignored the nature of asymmetric warfare. Hundreds of thousands of Vietcong and North Vietnamese soldiers were killed, but from 1965 to 1972 (the years America bore the brunt of the fighting), hundreds of thousands more poured into South Vietnam along the Ho Chi Minh trail. A body count was meaningless. The real determinant of North Vietnamese resolve was a ferocious desire for independence—a passion that long predated America's involvement and continued with a short but vicious border conflict with China.

Given these complexities, technology is a stopgap measure at best. It can hold the line, but only for so long. Today, it may help uncover terrorist cells. It may assist in destroying Al-Qaeda, but it cannot deal with root causes. In the Middle East, technology cannot defuse the tensions and pressures triggered by repressive governments, failed economic policy, and religious zealotry. In the United States, facts alone cannot explain how a group of Yemeni Americans, men raised in upstate New York, could become so alienated with American society as to give their allegiance to Osama bin Laden in Afghanistan. Understanding that decision, addressing the alienation that inspired it, is a much more complex process.

"INSTANTANEOUS DEMOCRACY"

In post-war Iraq, if the citizenry does not lust for freedom as the oppressed nations of Eastern Europe lusted when the Soviets crumbled, it's because they do not yet comprehend freedom or democracy or life without the heel of oppression on their necks. Here again, speed feeds instability. A culture grounded in ancient religious and tribal loyalties vanished in a matter of weeks. (After World War II, it took Japan a full generation to evolve from an ethnocentric, warlike nation.) At best, Iraqi knowledge of democracy is incomplete and wildly incoherent—bits and pieces of information flowing across airwaves and telephone lines creating static and distortion rather than clarity. Incomplete information (America must accept its share of responsibility for this enormous cultural gulf) feeds suspicion, insecurity, and prejudice, not hope or understanding.

Ultimately, Iraq's fate will not be decided by Americans, diehard Saddam Hussein supporters, or Islamic guerillas making jihad. It lies in the hands of the Iraqi people, so oppressed and brutalized they cannot tolerate "instantaneous" democracy any more than a prisoner freed from a dungeon can tolerate the light of day. (Americans, by contrast live in a world where change is constant, often welcome.) The children of Iraq, who instinctively flock to the GIs, whose faces glow in news photos against a backdrop of freshly painted classrooms and textbooks cleansed of propaganda, are a better barometer.

Despite our best intentions, the collision of such opposite cultures is inevitably traumatic, triggering debilitating rounds of elation and dashed hope. To an American, the toppling of Saddam Hussein's statue in Baghdad's Paradise Square on April 9, 2003, was familiar, rooted in our quicksilver culture. Presidents, Hollywood idols, CEOs, and football coaches routinely suffer similar fates. For us, Saddam's fall and his surrender to American soldiers in December 2003 crystallized the hope that the threat of terror (particularly chemical and biological terror) had been dispelled. To the average Iraqi, it was a terrifying leap into the unknown.

The ensuing chaos—looting, bombings, power outages, water

shortages, assassinations, Sunni-Shiite tensions, guerilla-style attacks—exacerbated the insecurities of both nations. In Iraq, a language barrier became an information barrier. Without words, explanations could not be made, good intentions communicated, cultural norms explained. In May 2003, the *Chicago Tribune*'s Liz Sly reported: "America's occupation of Baghdad is less than a month old, but already attitudes are souring among many Iraqis toward the troops they initially welcomed as liberators. . . . Iraqis say their joy at being freed from his [Saddam Hussein's] repressive regime is being replaced by fear, frustration, and fury at the Americans for not moving faster to replace the institutions they destroyed. 'We don't have jobs, we don't have a government, we don't know what our future is and we don't have safety,' Mansour Abdullah Hassoon, 32, an engineer with a state-run firm told Sly."

What was believed to be random violence committed by remnants of Saddam's Iraqi army was unmasked as orchestrated asymmetric warfare. Raw data, rumor, half-truths, speculation, the flotsam and jetsam of the Information Age, flooded in and out of the country. By the winter of 2004, this flow, coupled with casualty reports, the bombing of U.N. headquarters, the assassination of the moderate Shiite ayatollah, Mohamad Baqir al Hakim, had taken on a life of its own, sometimes at odds with reality.

It may well turn out that the threat posed by Saddam Hussein to his own people and the United States could not have been ignored. That does not make the struggle for the hearts and minds of both nations easier. "Only exceptional people tolerate change well," Mike Kami reminds us. "For the rest of humanity, the past, whatever that past may be, will always seem more secure." "We welcomed the Americans," Baghdad engineer Mansour Abdullah Hassoon told the *Chicago Tribune*. "We want to love them. But people are beginning to say Saddam was better than America."

It would be pointless to tell a suffering man trapped between two warring cultures that his statement is illogical. Yet, that apparently was the expectation. We must remind ourselves that we live in an interconnected world. People are starving. Children are dying of preventable illnesses. Terrorists are on the move. It seems equally pointless to remind Americans who argue that because there have been no terrorist attacks in the United States since September 11th, the threat has passed. Terrorists are patient. Eight years passed between the first bombing of the World Trade Center in 1993 and the final attack. Predators are cunning, without qualms or doubts. It's not surprising to discover that Saddam's partisans are bombing the power stations and pipelines supplying their own people. Not surprising that Al Quada may well be planning another attack on the U.S.

CHAPTER 29

The Information Storm

It is hardly surprising that the information storm—Western music, mores, fashion, trends, consumerism, ideology—streaming across the Third World is building fear and rage in some people groups, the root causes of terrorism. From their perspective, we've unleashed a tidal wave that's washing away their small towns and uprooting their ways of life that, in many respects have been unchanged for centuries.

Man's irrationality in the face of dramatic technological change is perhaps the greatest irony. The Islamic fundamentalists who claim they want to remove themselves from the corrupt influences of the West bob like corks in the flood of Western technology and ideas. In Afghanistan, the Taliban banned television, but hung the forbidden sets from the trees of Kabul like ripe fruit in the Garden of Eden. We are as powerless to halt this flood as the developing world is to hold it back. The tide is rising, the consequences, both positive and negative, will be enormous.

This reality will not fade away or respond to military force. It runs deeper than the battlefields of Afghanistan and Iraq. Information can describe, but not banish hunger, disease, illiteracy, and despair. What is required lies far beyond the scope of technology: a long-term, multi-national, multicultural commitment, in effect, a twenty-first century Marshall plan, dedicated to reversing decades of decay on one side; and studied indifference to the needs, politics and problems of the developing world on the other.

GOOD VS. BAD INFORMATION

Information is vital to this outreach, information that must flow in both directions. Like the architects of British Empire in the eighteenth and nineteenth centuries, we've remained ignorant, often oblivious to the developing world. In the decades after World War II, our attention was, understandably, on the Soviets and the Chinese. Third World nations and cultures were often perceived "dominoes" and proxies to be "played" by the superpowers and then abandoned. The chaos in Afghanistan after the Soviets' withdrawal opened the door to the Taliban and Al-Qaeda. Unlike the British who ruled their world unchallenged, we cannot make arrogance and insensitivity virtues.

In the 1960s and 1970s, technology both fueled and banked the flames that threatened to turn the Cold War into nuclear conflagration. Technology birthed tens of thousands of nuclear warheads deployed in submarines, hardened missile silos, and the bellies of globe-girdling bombers. On the other hand, *knowledge* of that destructive power held the superpowers to a standoff for more than two decades. At times, this uneasy peace frayed to a thread, but held. Today, mutual assured destruction is an incentive to the self-proclaimed martyrs of the new millennium. In 2004, who can imagine the atomic bomb as a peacekeeper?

During the Cuban Missile Crisis of October 1962, the world teetered on the brink of Armageddon because of a "failure to communicate." In its aftermath, a telegraphic "hotline" was installed between Washington and the Kremlin to limit any future snafus. Today, that same strength is also a weakness; the power to communicate instantaneously, whether in the hands of a terrorist or criminal, creates risk.

The Cold War ended because information proved more effective than saber rattling. Word of the clear and shining superiority of the Western economies, technology, and quality of life—television broadcasts, smuggled books, and Beatles' music—tamed the Russians, not the clash of armor in the Fulda Gap, not MIRV missiles, or Ronald Reagan's proposed Star Wars expenditures. The cornucopia of Western supermarkets, a marvel we take for granted, jarred the population of a world of barren stores, outmoded factories, and wretched living conditions into demanding something better—a hunger so basic it swept away Communism like the dust gathered on unread books. Today, the former Soviet republics are still struggling to bridge this gap.

As I write these words, news arrives of another round of suicide bombings and retaliatory attacks in Jerusalem, Tel Aviv, and the West Bank, another sign that Israelis and Palestinians on the U.S.-proposed "road map to peace" have come to another harrowing precipice. Among the victims, an Israeli emergency room doctor named David Applebaum, who made the mistake of visiting a cafe and sharing a coffee and some fatherly advice with his daughter Nava on the eve of her wedding. Nava died with her father; her wedding dress became a funeral shroud. Information alone cannot end this kind of horror. If it could, the sheer intensity of such images would drive hatred from the world.

I must also say we've not begun to approach the limits of what information *can* achieve. Earlier I cited a 2002 Pew Research Center survey that described the United States' image as having been tarnished all across the globe. The polls suggested this animosity is being stirred not only by our foreign policy, but our business practices, customs, ideas, and our fundamental notion of democracy itself. However disheartening, this is information that must be acted upon. We must redouble our efforts to understand the world around us—in our schools as much as in our State Department. This was the driving vision of my fellow Atlantan Ted Turner, who insisted on banishing the world "foreign" from all CNN newscasts. Only then, will the bad information upon which so much anti-Americanism is based be driven out by good information.

TRAPPED IN THE MIDDLE

It's hard to imagine, but similar animosity flared in the American heartland in the 1980s. It was defused but not without cost. Like the mindless hatred directed at the United States (the "Great Satan"), this outbreak was tied to misunderstanding, fear, and suspicion. Unlike the social upheavals of the 1960s, radicals or political extremists did not trigger the anger. It sprung from the most conservative segment of the American population, the farmer. It should have been anticipated. Between 1980 and 1990, *one million* family farms went bankrupt, caught in a whirlwind of escalating interest rates and diminishing crop prices. Most of the families who ran these farms had worked the land in Arkansas, Colorado, Kansas, Oklahoma, North Dakota, and Nebraska for generations. Many of these cautious men had been encouraged to borrow to accumulate as much acreage as they could in anticipation of an expected surge in international demand for grain and foodstuffs. Good times were promised to Middle America.*

That promise never materialized, in part, because sophisticated

American technology had been exported to Asia and South America, transforming agrarian countries with the advantage of cheap labor into fierce competitors. Many farmers watched their land and their livelihoods disappear at auctions held on county courthouse steps, often when they were producing record harvests. So it was not surprising that domestic extremists targeted these desperate farmers, giving the same kinds of explanations and making the same kind of promises one imagines Hamas and Al-Qaeda leaders make to their disciples. Cash-strapped farmers were encouraged to ignore their taxes, to declare bank debt null and void because "biblical law" forbade lenders from charging interest, to file nuisance lawsuits to clog the judicial system, to attack greedy agribusiness operators. From there, it was a short leap to proclaiming that "satanic" traitors were running the government in Washington, a "New World Order" was looming, NATO and the Trilateral Commission would orchestrate the destruction of the nation. These fears were inflamed by word of the federal government's assaults at Waco and Ruby Ridge. The resulting violence—committed by a tiny fringe faction who justified their acts as "God's will"—is analogous to what we're seeing in the Middle East* where a relatively small number extremists are claiming to speak for the vast religion of Islam.

It culminated on April 19, 1995, when two disaffected Gulf War veterans, Timothy McVeigh and a farm boy named Terry Nichols, detonated a massive ammonium nitrate and fuel oil bomb (the formula readily available on the Internet) outside the Alfred P. Murrah Building in Oklahoma City. How ironic that these alienated men used fertilizers developed to increase the richness and bounty of the earth to kill 167

---

* It may be a stretch on my part, but there is something to the notion of being trapped *in the middle*. In the 1980s, the small farmer laboring in the heartland was left behind as the East Coast and West Coast cultures evolved largely into information economies. The Middle East, an ancient culture with its highly evolved yet underemployed professional classes of bureaucrats, engineers, medical practitioners, and intellectuals, is caught in the grinding gap between the technologically advanced West and the largely agrarian civilizations of much of Africa, the Indian subcontinent, and Asia.

men, women, and children and maim hundreds more.

Prosecuting the farm radicals and exposing their twisted ideology in the courts and the media did not end the threat. It would take almost twenty years of determined law enforcement efforts, retraining, educational and community assistance programs before the rage sweeping through the heartland began to abate. Today, farmers are still struggling to come to terms with the fact that the small family farm, like the small town, is fading into history. The farms will inevitably give way to the high-tech agribusiness. Change, particularly rapid change, is never easy.

Knowledge may counter, but not break the cycle of broken families, poverty, and dysfunction that underlies so much self-destructive and antisocial behavior. To be effective, information must be used in concert with far-reaching public policy initiatives that reflect the best of America's academic, public, and private sector. If justice is served by building more prisons, it also demands day-care centers, magnet schools, and scholarships for those struggling to move up in society.

CHAPTER 30

The Genie in the Bottle

Even in ancient times, the relationship between man and machine was uneasy. In the *Iliad*, when a gigantic mechanical horse appeared at the gates of Troy, the priest Laocoon warned his fellow citizens to be wary of "Greeks bearing gifts." A warning, Homer tells us, that fell on deaf ears. (A modern parallel: intelligence that Middle Eastern terrorists intended to hijack airliners was ignored by the authorities.) Uncertainty has always accompanied the genie out of the bottle. We know the nuclear reaction harnessed to generate electricity can be used to wreak unimaginable havoc, that our thirst for oil holds us hostage to terror and tyrants—yet our demands for power are unabated. We know the information used to detect a terrorist can trample the innocent man's civil rights. We love technology; we use it freely, but find it deeply unsettling.

Mike Kami says this contradiction can be explained in a phrase:

humans are not equipped to deal with the changes that rapid techno-logical advance engenders. Technology exerts tremendous G-forces on fragile souls and psyches. Kami, who was present at the birth of the computer, has watched the gap between technology and the average person's ability to comprehend technology widen.

Technology is value-neutral. Throughout history it has been mar-shaled to both elevate and debase the human condition. Information, the most rapidly evolving and pervasive technology, is equally adept at uncovering the terrorist cell or invading the privacy of an innocent cit-izen. Truth (and here I mean raw, unfiltered data) can blind rather than illuminate. Humans grasp this duality intuitively; it's gut-wrenching.

This unease with technology has been a subtext of history, myth, religion, and literature. Troy burned. Icarus built wings made of feath-ers and wax and died trying to fly too close to the sun. (Want a mod-ern parallel? Look at the criticism of the space shuttle program in the aftermath of the *Columbia* disaster.) Dr. Faustus gave his soul to the devil in exchange for knowledge and information. His belated cry, "I'll burn my books!" came too late to save him. To George Orwell, Big Brother's eye was all seeing. The robots in Arnold Schwarzenegger's *Terminator 3: Rise of the Machines* once served man; now they want to annihilate mankind.

Theoretically, Kami argues, this gap cannot expand infinitely. At some crossroads between evolution and history, man will either master technology or erase himself from the planet. For the moment, com-pressed by meager life spans and the mistaken paths humans have fol-lowed throughout history, this dissonance can paralyze. "The majority of people are terrified of change," says Kami. "Sweeping policy changes, change of habits, lifestyles, comfort levels." In the worst case, he says, the kind of induced paralysis cedes the advantage of technol-ogy to those—Hitler and Stalin come immediately to mind—who would not hesitate to use it for destructive purpose.

Every application of technology carries the potential for abuse. It cannot be eliminated, just as the onrush of information can no longer be slowed. "You cannot reduce the potential for evil to zero," says Kami. "Attempting that, you block all that is good. Our best and brightest minds must be engaged to determine the policies that harness technology effectively and responsibly."

THE SPIRIT ANIMATES THE MACHINE

Ultimately, the technologies we've discussed are nothing more than fingers in a dike holding back a rising tide of despair, frustration, misunderstanding, and rage. The tremendous velocities at which technology now drives the world are creating unforeseen, even catastrophic risk—threats that can poison all the good that flows from scientific advance.

Technology is powerful, but like the Wizard of Oz, ultimately an illusion. The Tin Man understood that a machine must be powered by the compassion and understanding that resides within the human heart. Like the Tin Man, we cannot rest until that linkage is forged. The spirit not the machine must animate our domestic and international policies. We need information to build a better world. Not surveillance cameras and databases, but knowledge that can help staunch the wounds of bleeding nations, understanding that can bring down barriers and promote our common blessings—first among them our common humanity. Progress is being made, but there is still far too much risk, too much pain and fear in the world to suggest that the march of the Information Age has led us to the verge of the Promised Land.

By no means can one book begin to capture the entire scope of the issues discussed here. Developing the solutions should be left to another day and another forum, too. But, there are real, practical steps that can be taken to resolve the conflicts before us.

The proof is in the past. Our nation has always risen to such challenges, always marshaled the will and moral courage to act decisively in times of crisis. As history makes clear, it has never been easy and never without doubt or terrible cost. Material success and wealth do not define the American Dream. It is the willingness to rally, to sacrifice, and to endure in the pursuit of what is good and just.

We are at the dawn of the Risk Revolution; the final outcome has not been determined. We still have the ability to choose our course—the next great advance in society or a period of symbolic and literal conflict. Either way, the time to act is now.

EPILOGUE

I've always been aware of the clock. Growing up in Sayville . . . in my career . . . on a spiritual level, the clock that ticks for all of us. In the short span of my life, momentous things—man's first tentative steps into outer space . . . the dismantling of the Berlin Wall . . . the decline and fall of the Soviet Empire—have come to pass. I've tasted the bitter fruit of uncertainty and delay. Standing amid the smoke and rubble of the World Trade Center, I watched the wind scatter the dust of stolen lives. And I came closer still, compelled to bear witness to such monumental loss. My company operates Bode Technologies, one of the forensic DNA labs charged with identifying the remains of World Trade Center victims, an undertaking no one could have ever foreseen. I watched our young technicians power-up the technology that reads the innermost map of human existence. With reverence, they handled the orange-capped tubes containing thousands of charred bone fragments. I felt their fierce desire to bring closure to families and loved ones. And found myself drifting toward home.

Sayville remains a timeless place. The town looks much like it did when I was a boy except for a neon bracelet of outlet stores and family restaurants along the Montauk Highway. The bay still sparkles in the morning sun, still reflects the silver of the evening sky.

The memories stirred during my last visit once again reminded me of all that is good about small-town America. I realized that over the years, as my world expanded, I was constantly connecting with exceptional men and women drawn from small towns and rural communities, driven as so many of us are by the small-town person's hunger for connection with the larger world.

As I walked the familiar streets and registered familiar faces, it also struck me that so much that has happened since I left Sayville is a cir-

cle. That perhaps, the best parts of small-town existence—the sense of trust and familiarity and security—can be recreated. That information can turn stranger to friend . . . keep predators at bay . . . protect our children and loved ones. That with God's help, we could reset that ticking clock. This vision inspired me to write this book.

This and one thing more. Like the rest of America, Sayville has changed. Like Washington, D.C. and New York City, it has been violated. Three Sayville men, New York Fire Department battalion chief Richard Prunty, fireman Lincoln Quappe, and Brendan McCabe, an executive at Fiduciary Trust International, died in the World Trade Center. Their passing left a tear in fabric of Sayville that will take generations to repair. Like you, I will never forget that autumn's juxtaposed images of funeral corteges, grieving children, and sun-dappled streets. I didn't know these men except in the sense that perhaps as boys, we'd walked down Main Street, played on the same fields, rambled over the sandy beaches of the Great South Bay.

As small town men, we embraced the same dreams and hopes for our families. In that I knew them well.

INDEX